SEVEN GUIDES TO
Effective Prayer

SEVEN GUIDES TO
Effective Prayer

Colin Whittaker

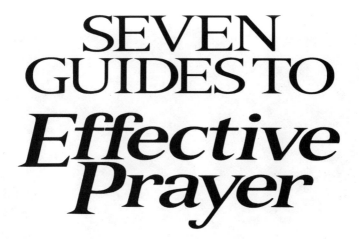

BETHANY HOUSE PUBLISHERS
MINNEAPOLIS, MINNESOTA 55438
A Division of Bethany Fellowship, Inc.

First published in Great Britain under the title, *Seven Great Prayer Warriors*, by Marshall Morgan and Scott Publications Ltd.

Copyright © 1987
Colin Whittaker
All Rights Reserved

Published by Bethany House Publishers
A Division of Bethany Fellowship, Inc.
6820 Auto Club Road, Minneapolis, Minnesota 55438

Printed in the United States of America

Library of Congress Cataloging-in-Publication Data

Whittaker, Colin G.
    Seven guides to effective prayer.

    Bibliography: p.
    1. Christian biography. 2. Prayer—Case studies.
I. Title. II. Title: 7 guides to effective prayer.
BR1702.W48   1988   248.3'2'0926   87-34106
ISBN 1-55661-011-4 (pbk.)

Dedication

This book is dedicated to the prayer warriors it
has been my privilege to find in every church I have
pastored. Particular mention must be made of my long-time
friend and first prayer-partner, Kenneth Reid of Rochdale.
The half-nights, nights, and days of prayer and fasting we
shared together throughout 1948–51, were more precious
than gold.

It is my joy to include in this dedication the growing
armies of prayer warriors which have arisen to bring down
the blessing of God on this generation: Women Aglow,
Lydia Fellowship, Coffee Pot Fellowship, Crusade for
World Revival, and Intercessors for Britain.

Contents

Preface

On my discharge from the Royal Army Medical Corps in 1947, after three-and-a-half years of National Service, a praying friend presented me with a copy of Finney's *Revival Lectures*. The inscription reads, 'With the sincere desire and prayer that you, Colin, may come to know more of Finney's Great God than he himself did'. As I prepared myself for the ministry in response to the call of God on my life, I devoured that book and every other one I could find on the subject of revival and prayer. Nearly forty years on I lament that I am a long way behind Finney and the other giants of God in this book. However, there is 'no discharge in this war' and I can only plead that I am pressing on toward the mark and still a willing if slow pupil in Christ's school of prayer. I have learned much: I have more to learn.

Throughout my thirty-eight years of Christian service in pastoring, writing and editing, these lives have inspired and instructed me. From them I have learned about the power of prayer and the importance of fasting. The one comparative newcomer in my life is Madame Guyon, about whom I must confess I knew little until I started on the research for this book. The decision having been made to include her, with after-thought I began to have serious misgivings and wonder whether I had made a mistake. However, long before I had finished researching Madame Guyon's life and writings, I was convinced of her right to link with the other six. Her pilgrimage to the truth and her path to prayer power make her worthy to rank with Luther. Thank God for such a woman. Praise God for women of like spiritual stature in our day who are at the forefront of spiritual warfare.

I have endeavoured to encapsulate faithfully the principal prayer features of these seven intercessors without any embellishment or personal comment, feeling that their lives speak for themselves. I believe everyone will find something in these lives to inspire them to seek afresh the face of God who answered their prayers and made them great. Not a few, I suspect, will also discover new depths of devotion and commitment which will seem strange when compared with our 'laid-back' praying in today's churches. In his classic on intercession, *The Power of Prayer and The Prayer of Power*, R A Torrey tells how, after he had used Brainerd's life as an example in a conference address, he was approached by a minister. It was Dr Park, the grandson and biographer of Jonathan Edwards. He commented, 'I have always felt that there was something abnormal about David Brainerd'. Dr Torrey replied, 'Dr Park, it would be a good thing for you and a good thing for me if we had a little more of that kind of abnormality'! In a fuller explanation Torrey said he meant 'the abnormality which bows a man down with intensity of longing for the power of God, that would make us pray in the way that David Brainerd prayed'.

I am greatly indebted to many authors and publishers for the sources of the material in this book and for permission to quote where necessary.

I must record my special thanks to Mr J Cowan, the present Director of Müller Homes, for giving me freely of his time and advice. The visit to the Bible College of Wales, founded by Rees Howells, was another rewarding experience. To meet his son, the saintly, gentle, and scholarly Samuel Howells, who succeeded his father, was a treasured occasion. My hours with his faithful colleagues, Dr Kingsley Priddy and Miss Doris Ruscoe, reliving their memories of prayer fellowship with Rees Howells, gave me a breath of the rarified heavenly atmosphere from the heights of intercession they scaled together with him. I am especially grateful to Dr Priddy for his invaluable help in the rewriting of the vital section of Rees Howells dealing with the period from December 1934 onwards. I am also grateful to Leslie T. Lyall for his gracious assistance with the checking of the section on Hudson Taylor.

Once again I am indebted to my agent, Edward England, for his wisdom and guidance; and to my publishers for their patience when my move to Bristol and return to pastoral life delayed the completion of this book. Not forgetting my daughter Beryl whose English teaching skills I increasingly appreciate; also my daughter-in-law Sheila, for retyping the final manuscript; both of them putting themselves out to help me at times when they were under extreme pressure with their own busy lives and families. Last, but not least, my helpmeet in every area of my life, my wife Hazel, for her patience in enduring yet again the endless clatter of the typewriter while I have been cloistered in my study with this book instead of with her!

Foreword

The hours I spent reading this manuscript—*Seven Great Prayer Warriors*—were some of the most richly rewarding hours of my life. It was sent to me by the author at a time when I was passing through a dark and difficult experience due to the death of my wife. Although my confidence in prayer had not been shaken I needed something to revitalise and refocus my personal prayer ministry. This book helped do it.

Who amongst us can honestly say that we do not need to be occasionally encouraged in relation to the matter of persevering prayer? I most certainly do. I am grateful for those times when someone has come alongside me and whispered, 'Keep going . . . God has more for you up ahead'.

I believe you will find this book a constant source of encouragement in your personal prayer life. These seven great personalities will come alongside you whenever you feel your feet flagging. Even now as I write phrases from the manuscript are still ringing in my mind like Hudson Taylor's famous statement, 'God's work done in God's way will never lack God's supplies'; and George Müller's equally famous remark, 'My eye is not on the thickness of the fog but on the living God who controls every circumstance of my life'.

We have so many books outlining the principles of prayer but so few on the practice of it. Whilst it is important to understand the principles of prayer it is equally important to observe how those principles are applied in human life and experience. Throughout the ages Bible teachers have taught that in order to be effective the study of prayer must be biographical. They claim that we cannot hope to catch the truth of so profound and personal a matter except as we watch and listen to men and women of prayer, to whom God was real, near and attentive. This book, giving as it does a glimpse into the prayer lives of some outstanding personalities of the past provides a worthwhile and valuable contribution to the study of both the principles and practice of prayer.

However, I know that one of two things can happen when one reads a book like this. One can be inspired, stretched and challenged. Or one can be overawed or daunted and say, 'I could never become such a passionate practitioner of prayer as these'. The latter need not happen if you keep in mind that God is not seeking to make you another 'Praying Hyde' or a 'Madame Guyon'—He wants you to be you. Take whatever challenge and truth that comes to you through these pages and allow God to weave it into the warp and woof of your life so that it enriches your personal prayer ministry and increases your spiritual potential. Don't let these great examples from the past daunt you—let them develop you.

For myself, I look forward to having this book alongside the others titles on prayer that are on my bookshelf to remind me of what fervent believing intercession can accomplish in this world and how mighty is the ministry of prayer.

Selwyn Hughes
Crusade for World Revival
September 1986

1: George Müller

Shrouded in thick fog off the coasts of Newfoundland, a
steamer edged slowly forward, its foghorn sounding out
mournful notes of warning. The captain, red-eyed from lack of
sleep and through peering vainly into the gloom, was startled
by a gentle tap on his shoulder. He swung round to find one of
his passengers—an old man in his late seventies, of tall,
dignified appearance, with impressive mutton-chop whiskers
and clear penetrating eyes. 'Captain,' he said, 'I have come to
tell you that I must be in Quebec on Saturday afternoon.' (It
was then Wednesday). The captain thought he detected a
slightly foreign accent in the voice, and he snorted his reply:
'Impossible'—he also resented the intrusion of a passenger in
the sanctity of the bridge. 'Very well,' was the calm response,
'if your ship can't take me, God will find some other means to
take me. I have never broken an engagement in fifty-seven
years.' The man's tranquility calmed the ruffled and tired
captain and he lifted his weary hands in a gesture of despair as
he replied, 'I would help if I could—but I am helpless'. His
hackles rose again as the old man suggested, 'Let us go down
to the chart room and pray.' The captain looked at him as
though he had just escaped from a lunatic asylum to make
such a ridiculous suggestion. 'Do you know how dense the fog
is?' he demanded. Without demurring the passenger
responded, 'No, my eye is not on the thickness of the fog but
on the living God who controls every circumstance of my life.'

The captain found himself unaccountably following the old
man into the chart-room and kneeling with him in prayer.
With childlike simplicity the man lifted his voice to God in a

prayer which the captain thought to himself more suited to a young Sunday school class than their fog-bound predicament. 'O Lord, if it is consistent with thy will, please remove this fog in five minutes. Thou knowest the engagement thou didst make for me in Quebec on Saturday. I believe it is thy will.' The captain (a nominal Christian) thought he had better humour the old man and was just about to pray when once again he felt a tap on his shoulder. He opened his startled eyes and blinked in mingled astonishment and resentment as he was commanded, 'Don't pray, because you do not believe, and as I believe God has already answered there is no need for you to pray.' The captain gulped and began to wonder who was the one in charge of the ship, but there was an air of calm authority about this man that compelled respect. He went on, 'Captain I have known my Lord for fifty-seven years and there has never been a single day that I have failed to gain an audience with the king. Get up, captain, and open the door, and you will find the fog is gone.' The captain duly obeyed, he flung it open and was amazed and astounded to find that the fog had disappeared.

The captain testified that his encounter with the aged and revered George Müller completely revolutionised the whole of his Christian life. From that moment faith became a reality to him and he knew that Müller's God was the true and living God. Yet there had been no promise of anything good in Müller's boyhood years. He looked more likely to turn out to be a criminal than one of the greatest Christians of his generation. A Prussian by birth, which was on the 27th September 1805 in Kroppenstaedt, near Halberstadt, his father was an excise collector who spoiled both George and his younger brother by over-indulging them, especially where money was concerned. The family moved to nearby Heimersleben when George was five years old. His father's position meant that there were frequently various amounts of government money lying around the house and young George (not content with his more than plentiful pocket money) early learned to purloin some of this for himself. Suspicions were aroused and his father set a trap, leaving nine-year-old George alone in a room with a pile of money. At the first opportunity he darted across the room, stuffed some money into his shoe, and returned to his place. As soon as his father came back he counted the money and confronted his thieving son. Unfortunately, far from being the end of his stealing, George played on his father's weak indulgence and grew up into his teens not only a cheat and a thief but a rebel and a renegade of the worst kind. He drank to excess, gambled, and on his own confession declared that there was scarcely a sin which he did not commit during his school and college years.

His father's ambition was for George to become a minister in the state church, a position which carried both prestige and a living good enough to ensure not only George's future but his own as well—in old age. With this in mind, when he was about ten years of age, George had been sent to the Halberstadt cathedral school. It was a good school—but not for the young Müller. By the time he was fourteen he was regularly drinking to excess and gambling at cards. When his mother died and his father came to break the unexpected and sad news he was shocked to find fourteen-year-old George the worse for drink. Unfortunately, even the burial of his mother failed to halt George's mad rebelliousness and he returned to school to pursue his downward course with renewed intensity. Nothing was sacred to him. He cheated church and chums without a qualm. The night before his confirmation he indulged in gross sins and then cunningly defrauded the clergyman out of most of the fee which his father had entrusted to his keeping for the purpose.

Throughout his teens George went from bad to worse. At sixteen he set off on a tour, staying at expensive hotels, (often with a woman) and then leaving with his bills unpaid. He had a passionate affair with a young Roman Catholic girl whom he had met soon after his confirmation. Time after time he got away with his 'playboy' style escapades but in Wolfenbuttel things finally caught up with him. He slipped away from the hotel without paying but this time he was caught and brought back. Unable to pay, his pleas for mercy fell on deaf ears and he was jailed. To make matters worse it was the festive season and here he was at sixteen, a criminal, sharing a cell with another thief. He languished there for three and a half weeks, from December 18th 1821 to January 12th, until his father heard of his plight, settled the unpaid hotel bills and by paying the other costs involved, managed to get him sent home. George's indulgent father for once tried to remonstrate seriously with him and for a short time it seemed to work. George got down to some hard study which pleased his father who began to think that he had learned his lesson. But it was short-lived; he was soon back to his old ways, deceiving and stealing from his father and from his friends. In spite of everything the plan was still for George to enter the ministry and he enrolled at Nordhausen in October 1822 to study the classics. He remained there for two-and-a-half years and outwardly he appeared to be reformed but secretly he carried on in his old ways. George's way of life threatened to undermine his health and he suffered several long illnesses, mainly attributable to his various excesses, which also reduced him to constantly being in debt. A bare-faced liar, he even resorted to staging a fake robbery, pretending that his trunk had been broken open and his money stolen. Nevertheless he was accepted as a candidate for the Lutheran ministry with permission to preach and to study at Halle University. He tried to reform but only because he realised that if he was to make a good living as a clergyman he would need a good degree and a somewhat better reputation. It was useless and George was soon reduced to having to pawn his watch and his clothes to pay his many debts. In spite of lack of funds he planned a six-week tour of the Swiss Alps with three of his new friends from Halle University. He stopped at nothing; to obtain their passports George persuaded his friends to forge letters purporting to be from their parents. Throughout the trip, George handled the common purse for the party and he cheated them shamelessly so that they paid (unknowingly) a good proportion of his dues.

After the summer vacation of 1825 George returned to his studies at Halle University, as ignorant as ever about the things of God. He had not read his Bible for years and did not have one with him. Almost three-quarters of the 1260 students at Halle were divinity students, but the great majority of them were unenlightened spiritually and—like Müller—without any personal experience of the saving power of Christ. One exception happened to be a young man called Beta who had accompanied Müller on the Swiss Alps tour and had been led astray by him. Beta was so convicted after the trip that he confessed his backsliding to his father who had put him in touch with a Mr. Wagner who held a regular meeting for prayer and Bible reading at his house in Halle. Beta told George that he was going to this meeting on Saturday evening and to his surprise George expressed a desire to accompany him. It was the last thing Beta expected; such a meeting seemed the last place the notorious card-playing, wine-drinking, dance-loving Müller would want to attend. Müller himself wondered why he felt this urge to go, but when Beta called for him on that all important Saturday evening in November 1825, he was ready. Any embarrassment at being in such unusual company was swept away by the warm welcome Mr Wagner gave him: 'Come as often as you please! House and heart are open to you.'

That evening the love of God reached down into the prodigal's heart through that little company of true believers. After the singing of a hymn, one man dropped to his knees and prayed. The sight and sound of that kneeling figure transfixed young Müller. It was the first time in his twenty-one years that he had seen any one on his knees praying—the Prussian habit was to stand when praying in public. A reading from the Bible followed and then a printed sermon was read (preaching in such a gathering being banned in those days except by an ordained clergyman). Mr Wagner closed the meeting with prayer and Müller wondered how it was that a man with an inferior education could pray in a way far superior to anything he himself was capable of. Furthermore there was a strange sense of joy springing up inside him which he could not account for in any rational way. That night as he lay down to sleep a new peace enfolded him. Three times that following week he returned to Mr Wagner's house to search the Scriptures. Quietly, undramatically, but with devastating reality the mysterious wind of God's Spirit had touched Müller's sinful, selfish heart resulting in an amazing new birth. His life was changed and as he fellowshipped with the little group of believers his evil habits and lifestyle were quickly altered. He made no secret of his new found faith and he was ridiculed and mocked by some of the students. It was the love of God in Christ that won him and from the first he found the twin pillars of the Bible and prayer, on which his life would be built.

George started the new year of 1826 with a desire in his heart to become a missionary, but a growing friendship with a young lady in the group began to cool this ambition. For some six weeks his new-found zeal for God continued to decline until one of the group, Hermann Ball—who came from a wealthy family—announced his intention of giving up all his wealth in order to take the gospel to the Jews in Poland. This sacrifice challenged George and he responded by yielding up his friendship with the girl in question and renewing his consecration to Christ. It was costly but his desire to become a missionary blazed up afresh in his heart.

George soon wrote to his father and brother seeking to share his new found faith with them but instead of being pleased his father was angry. Consequently George knew when the time came for him to approach his father about becoming a missionary that it would not be easy. He was right—his father did everything he could to dissuade him. George realised that if he was not going to do what his father wanted then it was wrong to continue taking his support at university. He determined to trust God for provision and refused his father's support. Back at Halle George soon realised the seriousness of the step he had taken and took the matter before God in prayer. He had to do two more years to complete his studies but he soon proved the faithfulness of God. Some Americans were studying in Halle and wanted a tutor to teach them and engaged George. The pay was sufficient to see him through the remainder of his time at university. Not only that, but three of them were college professors, and one of them none less than Charles Hodge who was destined to become so famous at Princeton. The fellowship with such men was an added bonus.

George was still a babe in Christ and had much to learn. He became so impatient about the missionfield that he tried to hurry things along by drawing lots in order to find out where God wanted him. George's idea was to buy a ticket in a lottery and he decided that if he won a prize he would take it as a sign that God wanted him to go; if not, then he should stay at home! He won a small prize and accordingly applied to the Berlin Missionary Society but was not accepted because he did not have his father's consent. George eventually learned that God does not guide in this way and put such elementary mistakes behind him as he eagerly pursued his new life as a Christian (although twice more he resorted to using the lot as a means of guidance, again with most unsatisfactory results so that he forever abandoned it).

By writing letters to his former friends, distributing tracts, and witnessing personally whenever possible, George began to learn the secrets of successful service. He succeeded in winning a schoolteacher for Christ. The man lived a few miles away from Halle, and he invited George to come and preach in the parish. It was his first attempt at preaching and George decided that the way to do it was to memorise a published sermon by someone else. He recited it twice—at the 8.00 am service and then the 11.00 am worship. However, when they asked him to preach again in the afternoon he was forced to pray desperately for God's help as he had no fresh material. He chose to read Matthew chapter five and endeavoured to expound it. No sooner had he begun to speak on the first beatitude than he was conscious of a new liberty; the word of God opened itself to him and he was enabled to convey his message so simply and effectively that the congregation gave him their undivided attention. On his way back to Halle he rejoiced and realised that God had revealed to him that this was the true way to preach. Even so it took George some considerable time to become a really effective expounder of the Scriptures and he was disappointed over the little fruit from his early efforts.

The first period of George Müller's Christian life was by no means perfect. He frequently studied for fourteen hours a day as he had a lot of lost time to make up for, but it took its toll and he suffered from nervous depression. Consequently his experience went through quite a few ups and downs. His prayer-life was by no means constant and on one dark day he tried to drown his sorrows in drink, but God was merciful to him and he found that his capacity for drinking had already so diminished that just a few glasses of wine were all he could manage—his appetite for such had really gone. Gradually, mainly through the warm fellowship of the little group of half-a-dozen or so at Mr Wagner's house, George was built up in his faith.

Various missionfields seemed to tug at his heart as he continued to seek God about his future sphere of service, but eventually a suggestion by George's godly tutor, Dr Tholuck, that he should consider working among the Jews, found a ready response. He applied and was invited to come to England for six months for training with the London Society for Promoting Christianity among the Jews. March, 1829 saw him sailing for London having overcome, through prayer, a number of seemingly insurmountable obstacles— including the fact that the Prussian Army required him to do national service. Müller's faith was rising.

In London George studied hard to master the Hebrew language but he was always more eager to get out among the Jews of London and witness to them. After only two months he became ill and in the providence of God was sent down to Teignmouth on the Devon coast to recuperate. Here he met some of the founders of the Brethren movement, including Henry Craik, a Scotsman who was to become his closest friend. Müller said that what happened to him then was like a second conversion. The first four years of his Christian life had been very weak. He confessed that during that period he had read very little of the Bible, preferring to read tracts or other books before the Word of God. July 1829 was the turning point which brought him to accept the Scriptures as the only guide and standard of judgment in spiritual things. He made a fresh and total surrender of his life to the Lord Jesus. After this the Word became his priority and over the following years he read the Bible from cover to cover more than one hundred times with prayer and meditation!

The truth of the Lord's second coming was also unfolded to George through Henry Craik. When he returned to London in September 1829 he was a renewed person. He started a prayer meeting among his fellow students from six to eight every morning, and frequently they prayed together in the evenings.

That summer witnessed the total consecration of George Müller. Everything: honour, pleasure, money, physical powers, intellect, were all laid at the feet of Christ. Asked the secret of his life he once replied, 'There was a day when I died, utterly died, died to George Müller, his opinions, preferences, tastes and will; died to the world, its approval or censure; died to the approval or blame of even my brethren and friends—and since then I have studied only to show myself approved unto God.'

Throughout the remaining months of 1829 George prayed earnestly about his future and finally decided, after his several overtures to the Missionary Society had been turned down, that the time had come for him to become entirely independent and trust God for his future. He left London for Devon at the close of 1829. After three happy weeks in Exmouth during which he preached regularly and with some success, he went to the neighbouring town of Teignmouth to preach there. His preaching was beneficial to many, although George aroused some opposition which surprised him. He also preached for his new friend, Henry Craik, at Shaldon. After he had been in Teignmouth for three months the little group of some eighteen believers invited him to become their pastor. He accepted but made it clear that he felt that his future lay in itinerant ministry. It was now that he laid the foundation for the whole of his future ministry. As he began to expound regularly the Scriptures in the simplest possible way he found that his little flock was blessed and God also increased their numbers. His fellowship with Henry Craik, who was in close proximity, was a great enrichment to him.

Other vital truths presented themselves to George. He was challenged about believer's baptism. His initial reaction was hostile but after prayerfully examining the Scriptures he was fully persuaded that it was his duty to be baptised by immersion. Examination of the Bible also convinced him of the desirability of breaking bread every Lord's Day.

Another important event occurred when Müller was preaching at Exeter for there he met and fell in love with a charming Christian lady called Mary Groves, the sister of Anthony Norris Groves who was fast making a name for himself as an outstanding servant of Christ and a great missionary. She was eight years older than George but it was a perfect match and their marriage on October 7th 1830 was the beginning of a united life of mutual happiness and helpfulness in God's service. Soon after their marriage they agreed that it was right for them to trust God for their financial needs rather than continuing to receive the salary which was derived from pew rents. It was a bold step for a newly married couple and on more than one occasion their faith was sorely tried, but God never failed them and He was surely preparing them for the great task ahead.

After two years George's new friend and neighbour, Henry Craik, lost his young wife, and receiving an invitation to pastor a congregation in Bristol he went there for a month in March 1832. The needs of the great city led him to think of the possibility of George Müller joining him. They both prayed much about it. It was not an easy decision; Mary was expecting their first child in September and life in Teignmouth was pleasant. City life would be very different. On April 22nd 1832, George Müller preached in Gideon Chapel and in the afternoon in Pithay Chapel with a view to coming to Bristol. God sealed his ministry with the salvation of a young man who was a notorious drunkard. After further prayer George arranged to leave his congregation in Teignmouth at the end of May, and so began the joint ministry of these two friends and men of God. From the first God blessed their faithful ministry and the work prospered. Bethesda Chapel was rented for a year and services were held there as well as at Gideon Chapel. On August 13th, 1832 Müller and Craik and five others formally founded what they prayerfully purposed would be a simple New Testament church with the Word of God as their sole guide.

That summer cholera raged throughout the city with death and suffering everywhere. The two young ministers (George was only twenty-six) were kept busy night and day, visiting the dying, burying the dead, and praying for the plague to cease. It was not until October that it began to abate and then it soon became apparent what a trail of misery it had left behind, with many children orphaned and in great need of care and help. At the height of the epidemic Mary gave birth to their daughter, Lydia, on the 17th September.

In May 1833 a review of their first year in Bristol provided abundant evidence that it was the will of God they should be there. Over one hundred people had been added to the two works at Bethesda and Gideon Chapel. There were sixty-five definite conversions, as well as many backsliders restored. At first Henry Craik was a much more effective preacher of the gospel than Müller. As they dealt with inquirers on a one-to-one basis it was all too obvious that most of them attributed their conversion to Mr Craik's preaching. This led Müller into a prayerful examination of the reasons behind his friend's greater success in reaching the unconverted. He quickly realised that Henry was more spiritually minded; more earnest in prayer for converting power; and more direct in his approach. Müller immediately set himself to remedy his defects and made this a matter of special prayer, with the result that he soon became just as effective as Henry in his evangelistic preaching.

Both Henry and George had stipulated that they would not receive a salary from the church but would continue to look to the Lord to supply their needs through voluntary offerings from those to whom they ministered. The end of 1833 marked four years of living this way and Müller was able to record that God had been faithful and generous—the amount received having more than doubled in the four years, from £130 in 1829 to £267 in 1833. In turn he was generous and faithful in his own giving: Müller proved that he could be trusted with money as well as rely on God to supply it.

The Bible was now the supreme book in George's life, but three other books also made significant impressions upon him during his first decade of ministry. One book was the biography of A H Francke, who had founded a famous Christian Orphanage in Halle, Germany in 1696, which became during its time the largest in the world, caring for about 2,000 orphans. Francke operated on 'faith lines'—depending on God to supply the many needs of this great work. The other books were the biography of John Newton, the converted slave-trader, who became the writer of so many beautiful hymns and an outstanding preacher of the gospel of God's saving grace; and a biography of George

Whitefield, the great revivalist who was so signally used of God. The life of Newton greatly encouraged Müller because it was a parallel of his own in many ways, especially as an illustration of God's grace in changing a rebellious and wild young man; it also stirred him to start keeping his own journal of God's dealings in his life. From Whitefield, Müller learned that his success in soul-winning was especially linked with an unusually deep prayer life; and his understanding of spiritual things was largely due to a regular habit of reading the Bible on his knees—a method which Müller began to adopt with great profit, along with a renewed resolve to give himself to even more prayer.

The needs of the poor pressed heavily upon George Müller and in June 1833 he began to gather some of the poorest children in the neighbourhood for breakfast, followed by some teaching. He followed this with a similar programme to feed and teach adults and some of the aged poor. The attempt proved abortive, because after some initial success which revealed the need for some such programme, he ran into difficulties when the crowds of beggars attracted by the offer of free bread began to annoy the neighbours who complained very strongly.

Throughout 1833 God continued to bless Müller's and Craik's united labours and the number added to them now totalled 227 men and women, of which 125 belonged to Bethesda Chapel and 132 to Gideon Chapel. Although these two men of God were very firm in their convictions they were also very open to all true, born-again believers, in whose lives they saw the fruit of the Spirit. They felt a burden to help the cause of Christ wherever possible and this led to the founding on March 5th 1834, of the Scriptural Knowledge Institution for Home and Abroad. The fourfold aim of the Society was as follows:

1. To assist day schools, Sunday schools and adult schools in which instruction was given on Scriptural lines

2. To put the children of poor people into such day schools
3. To circulate the Holy Scriptures
4. To aid in supplying the wants of missionaries and missionary schools.

They both agreed that SKI (as it became affectionately known) would never ask for money; would use only committed Christians; would never go into debt; but would be sustained by faith in God through the means of secret prayer. From the very first God honoured their great step of faith and without any initial funds, and without any advertising, a stream of blessing started to flow which continued to increase in volume throughout the years. Yet at the time when this great project was launched, George recorded in his journal that he had only one shilling (5p in today's currency, or one twentieth of a pound), and furthermore, his wife Mary was well advanced in her second pregnancy. Just two weeks after the founding of SKI at a public meeting, Mary presented George with a son. There was only one possible name for him—Elijah, 'My God is Jah' (meaning Jehovah), for this name was one of George's life-mottoes.

The launch of such an Institution, coupled with the responsibility of a growing church, would have been sufficient for most men, but George found God burdening him more and more to do something on a permanent basis for the orphans. The conditions of the poor when Queen Victoria came to the throne were dreadful in the extreme. There was no free public education, no dole, no child allowance, no Factory Acts and inspectors, and next to no orphanages. In 1840 Lord Shaftesbury reminded Parliament that children of six and seven years were working twelve to fourteen hours a day in factories, in potteries, in coal mines, and were without any schooling. Orphans who managed to escape from the factories, lived on the streets, ragged and bare-footed, surviving mostly by stealing, compelled to sleep outside in winter and summer. Children who were sent to the poorhouses were hardly any better off; the conditions were cruel and the atmosphere corrupt. Wages generally were so low that it was well nigh impossible for families to feed the extra mouths of orphaned relatives; some bravely tried but had to virtually starve themselves to do so. In 1834 there were only 3,600 places for orphans in the whole of England, consequently some 7,000 children, eight years of age, were 'cared for' in the prisons—in conditions which were abominable.

George accordingly prayed more and more about starting an orphanage, looking to God for clear guidance in the matter. The church was continuing to flourish—only two-and-a-half years after George's coming to Bristol over two hundred had been added to their numbers, making a total membership of 257. The newly founded Scripture Knowledge Institute was also blossoming with a Sunday school of 120 children; an adult class of forty; four day schools with over two hundred children; hundreds of Bibles and New Testaments had been distributed; and £57 had been received and sent out for the support of missionary work. A total of £167 had been received for SKI by prayer alone (a sum worth many times more than today's currency: then a farm labourer's weekly wage was about ten shillings or half of one pound). The guidance George was seeking had not been long in coming.

One day, George's brother-in-law, Anthony Norris Groves, who had been a missionary since 1829, came home for a visit, and called on the Müllers in Bristol. Groves was anxious to visit Germany with a view to seeking workers to join him in his missionary work in India. George needed little persuading to join him on the trip which would give him a chance to see his father and brother, and so it was that in 1835 he found himself back home in Germany. He was grateful to find his father much softened in his attitude towards him and more open to the things of God; so much so that when the time came to say farewell his father declared, 'May God help me to follow your example, and to act according to what you have said to me.' Whilst in Halle he visited his old professor, Dr

Tholuck, and also was given the opportunity to see Francke's orphanage. The trip occupied about two months and soon after his return to Bristol, George and Mary faced a sore trial of their faith. First Mary's father died, and their children Lydia and Elijah were both very ill. Four days after the death of Grandfather Norris, little Elijah died and they were buried in the same grave.

It was a difficult time, funds were low and George's clothes were old and worn. He refused to borrow and believed that his Heavenly Father was well aware of such things and would provide. It was not long before he was given a new suit by a fellow believer. George's health was also suffering at this time; again the Lord undertook for them in the provision of a much needed holiday. Müller was fond of quoting 'The steps of a good man are ordered by the Lord' (Psalm 37: 23), sometimes adding 'and the stops'. The respite did him good but having time to reflect he was conscious of how much God still had to do in him regarding holiness.

On November 20th, 1835, Müller was having tea with a Christian lady and it just so happened that she had a copy of Francke's biography. The effect of this encounter, coupled with his recent visit to Francke's orphanage was deeply to convict George that God was clearly telling him to open up a similar orphanage and that the time had come for him not just to think about it but to set about doing it. The impression did not go away but rather increased. As he prayed the matter through Müller felt that God was not just calling him to imitate Francke but to provide a living example to Christians of the power of prayer that would strengthen their faith. He felt the need to prove to his generation that God is the Living God and is to be trusted because He is faithful. He wanted to care for the poor orphans, but even more he was concerned for the glory of God. His supreme motive was that God might be magnified by orphans being fully provided for in a Christian environment by prayer and faith alone.

George sifted his motives before God in prayer; he shared

his desires with Henry Craik that they might be tested, and his friend encouraged him to go ahead. On December 2nd, 1835, he took the first step by ordering printed notices announcing a public meeting on December 9th, when the plans for an orphanage would be laid before his fellow believers. During that week he was assailed by doubts but as he sought the face of God he was tremendously encouraged by the words in another Psalm, 'Open thy mouth wide and I will fill it' (81: 10). It stood out in such a way that he could never forget it and it became another of his great life-mottoes. At the public meeting although he was nervous at first, as soon as he began to speak he was very conscious that God was helping and inspiring him.

Müller subsequently prayed for £1,000, for good workers and for suitable premises. All were soon forthcoming. A poor woman who worked as a seamstress, earning only a few shillings, sent him £100—a large sum in those days for anyone, let alone one so poor. Müller took it upon himself to visit this generous giver and was deeply moved at the spirit of this godly woman. She had inherited the money but George was afraid that perhaps she was giving rashly and might afterwards regret it and want to change her mind. When he urged her to count the cost before finally deciding, she responded, 'The Lord Jesus has given His last drop of blood for me, and should I not give Him this £100?' This incident revealed not only the spirit of this woman which was typical of many more who sacrificially supported the work, but also the spirit of George Müller who never pressurised people in any way. The only pressure he ever sought to exert was by means of the throne of God through prayer.

Within five months George and Mary Müller, with the help of friends, began to furnish their own home at 6 Wilson Street in the St Pauls area of Bristol, preparing it to accommodate a maximum of thirty orphan girls. The Müllers moved out at the end of March and the rented house was formally opened with prayer and praise on the 21st April 1836. George had prayed for everything—the property, the staff, the finance, the furnishings but he had omitted to pray for the orphans—feeling sure that they would be overwhelmed by applications. Some days before the opening there was not a single application!—it would have been amusing if it had not been so serious. George was shattered; he flung himself on his face (literally) and lay all evening before God, praying and humbling himself under the hand of the Almighty. He eventually reached a position where he was willing for the whole scheme to come to nothing—if that was God's will and would be to His glory. The very next day the first application came, to be quickly followed by others and by May 18th there were twenty-six orphans in the house and more expected.

Things now began to move quite rapidly. The establishment of orphanages was added to the existing list of SKI's objectives. Before the end of the year they were able to open another house in the same street (1 Wilson Street) for infant orphans. George's faith was increasing all the time but it was tested and refined by many trials—not a few of which were very fiery indeed. In the early days especially they had to learn to live from hand to mouth, and from day to day; seldom did they have a surplus of funds. Gifts also tended to be in small amounts and came just when needed. This puzzled George at first and he was tempted to feel that it was on account of his personal failure in some area, but gradually he came to understand that God was teaching him that His provision catered for the minutest details, and though sometimes left until the last minute would never be late.

Such a life of trust provided an endless fund of marvellous stories of God's faithfulness in providing for their needs. Once dinner for the orphans was delayed for half an hour because of lack of provisions, but this was an almost unique occasion. Throughout the years the meals (though often quite plain and repetitive) were usually served right on time. One morning, the tables were all set for breakfast but the cupboard like that of the proverbial Mother Hubbard was bare, and so was the cash box. The children were standing waiting for their breakfast and Mr Müller said, 'Children, you know we must be in time for school'. Then lifting his head he prayed very simply, 'Dear Father, we thank Thee for what Thou art going to give us to eat'. There was a knock at the door. It was a local baker who said, 'Mr Müller, I could not sleep last night. Somehow I felt you didn't have any bread for breakfast, and the Lord wanted me to send you some. So I got up at 2.00 am and baked some fresh bread and here it is.' Mr Müller thanked the baker and praised God for His care. Then there was a second knock at the door. It was a milkman whose cart had broken down right outside the orphanage. He had come to unload his milk onto the orphans so that he could get his waggon repaired!

During this period Müller had several bouts of sickness and was sometimes unable to preach for a number of weeks. The church was still growing with about fifty new members being added every year. By 1837 their numbers had increased to about four hundred. In spite of the many calls upon him. Müller felt that his greatest need was to spend more time in prayer and this he determined to do, no matter what the cost. Because of his poor health he had taken to getting up a bit later and also he had started taking a little sleep after lunch, for about half an hour. Stirred by a chance remark about the Levitical sacrifices giving only the best parts to God, and the analogy that we ought to give the best part of our time to communion with Christ in prayer, he determined that at whatever cost to his health, he would get up earlier to pray, as well as cutting out that after-lunch nap. Far from his health suffering he testified to being much better and spiritually he was greatly enriched by long and precious sessions of prayer before breakfast. It was a habit he maintained throughout his long life, finding that he could manage on about seven hours sleep. He would rise at 6.30 am and devote himself to prayer and Bible reading until 7.45 am, when he started dealing with his heavy load of correspondence.

Müller never stopped learning; he was always willing to change if he felt this was the leading of the Holy Spirit. For some ten years the first thing he had done after rising and dressing was to give himself to prayer. He now felt that he should begin the day by giving himself to read the Word of God and to meditate prayerfully upon it. Within a few minutes he said that he found that he was led to confession, or thanksgiving, or intercession, or supplication. He searched the Bible with a view to 'feeding' his own soul and by breakfast time, with rare exceptions, he discovered that he was in a happy state of heart. This was something he constantly shared wherever he went, that the believer's first business at the beginning of the day was to get their soul into a state of happiness with the Lord. Müller also took to walking and praying—with his New Testament in his hand—when conditions were suitable. On occasions he made this his early morning devotions, walking, reading a New Testament in large type, meditating and praying, as he walked in the fields for between an hour or two hours before breakfast. Both his physical and spiritual health benefited from this method.

In George's journal he had the courage to bare his soul on many occasions, revealing that he was a man of similar passions to the rest of us and subject to his 'off days' when he was irritable with his wife, or with visitors who outstayed their welcome; he too had his battle with doubts and fears. His great secret was that he learned not only to pray but never to give up praying.

By 1837 there were eighty-one children in the three orphan houses, and nine staff. It was quite a family to feed by faith! Although he published an annual report, which was always eagerly looked for by supporters of the work, Müller never resorted to appeals of any sort and never asked anyone—except God—for help. Some tried to attribute the support received as a direct result of the report, but Müller never placed any dependence whatsoever upon the publishing of the reports to raise support. In fact, immediately after the annual public meeting, donations frequently fell to their lowest. On one occasion when they were in dire need and under great pressure, Müller deliberately delayed the publishing of the report so that when the answers to prayer came no-one would attribute it to the report instead of to a prayer-answering God.

The trials were often prolonged and the temperature of the furnace in which his faith was tried seemed to get hotter and hotter, but Müller accepted that trials are the food on which faith feeds and grows strong. The period of seven years ending in 1845 was a particularly difficult one. In the two years between August 1838 and August 1840 there were fifty occasions when they were reduced to being penniless, or without sufficient funds for the day, but God always undertook and either money or food came in time.

The increasing number of orphans they were accommodating forced Müller to begin praying seriously about the possibility of opening a fourth home—even though they were still passing through a period of testing and funds were still very low. In the middle of this time of difficulty one day as he stood in his room praying about the situation, he took a valuable diamond ring which had been given for the support of the orphanages and used it to etch on the windowpane the words 'Jehovah Jireh' (meaning 'the Lord will provide'). Many times as he looked out of the window those words reassured him and he was lifted up. In due time another house in Wilson Street became available (No. 4) and after praying the matter through and being convinced that it was the right thing to do, Müller took it. It was a real step of faith because he and his faithful staff had just about used every possible asset they had to keep the orphanages going. Everything that could be disposed of had been turned into cash, but George regarded it as a great challenge to his faith—and he accepted it. God did not fail him.

For the first ten years of the orphanages' existence Müller had had no thought of building, preferring to use existing properties which were available to rent. However, in October

1845, he received a polite but serious letter of complaint from a neighbour in Wilson Street. The growing number of children in the street was making it unpleasantly noisy for the rest of the people who lived there. He prayerfully considered it and was soon convinced that the neighbours did have some cause for complaint and perhaps the Lord was nudging him to consider that the time had come to move to more suitable premises in healthier and more open surroundings.

George was soon boldly praying that the Lord would find them seven acres of land on which they could erect a purpose-built orphanage to house three hundred children. Over the next five weeks he prayed continuously about this and when a letter came in December containing the largest gift he had ever received—one thousand pounds—he was certain that God was behind his plan.

Early in 1846 Müller heard about land being for sale on the Ashley Down area of Bristol—seven acres of it! George made plans to visit the owner but missed him on his first visit. This delay gave God a chance to convict the owner (who had already been informed of Müller's interest in the land). That night the landowner woke up at 3.00 am and unable to go back to sleep he found himself thinking about the sale. As he pondered the matter he decided that he would let Müller have the land if he applied for it, and instead of asking £200 per acre which was the original price he had fixed, he determined that he would let Müller have it for £120 per acre. Next morning when Müller called again he shared with him the story of his early awakening and what he had decided. Müller was delighted but by no means surprised at such a happening; he knew that it was the Lord who had awakened the man and spoken to him.

An architect in London volunteered to draw up the plans and superintend the building without any charge. This was another encouragement to Müller as he prayed for God to send in the large sums of money which would be needed for such an undertaking, but over the next five months he was tested again as very little came in for the new building. Then in July 1846 he received a gift of £2,050—by far the largest donation he had ever received. His heart was so full of joy that he threw himself down on the floor to lie flat on his face before the Lord; he burst forth in thanksgiving and surrendered his heart afresh to his Saviour. Between July 1846 and March 1849 they received £15,748 which was sufficient to pay for the building and furnishings of Number One Orphan House on Ashley Down. They moved from Wilson Street into the new premises in June, 1849, and by December it was full with three hundred children.

Müller was now convinced that the crying need of the thousands of orphans in the nation warranted another and still bigger building project. Along with his wife he prayed earnestly about the matter and together they had sufficient faith to ask for another building to accommodate seven hundred orphans. When a donation of £3,000 was received on January 14th 1851 George felt that God was putting His seal of approval upon it and set himself to pray the matter through. This he did many times daily over the next two years but again it was a trial of his faith as gifts came in very slowly. They came in steadily, almost every day, but it was a trickle compared with the large sum required. Then at last the break came with a joint donation from several Christians of £8,100. George's spirit rose in fresh thanksgiving to God for His faithfulness: he had come to realise from experience that it is through faith and patience we inherit the promises of God.

Eventually it was decided to build two smaller houses instead of one large one. The second Orphan House was opened in 1857 and the third in 1862. They had received the £35,000 needed and more besides, and were now able to accommodate 1,150 children. However, Müller was still unable to rest: there were far more orphans in the country than there were places for them in orphanages—although others such as Dr Barnado were now following Müller's example and taking up the challenge. The writings of Charles Dickens had also stirred up the conscience of the nation. The conditions of many establishments left much to be desired and Dickens toured the country exposing many of them for their cruelty and neglect. He paid a visit to Müller's homes and left very satisfied at what he saw. The conditions in the homes on Ashley Down were certainly not luxurious—Müller never believed in wasting the Lord's money—but they were clean and bright, the food plain but adequate. In fact, generally speaking Müller's homes were in advance of their times. He was even accused by some critics of giving the orphans too good an education and giving them ideas above their station in life! Others said that by keeping the boys until they were fourteen and the girls until they were seventeen he was robbing the factories of labour. Things were not perfect, of course; Müller freely admitted that they had made their mistakes and had their share of disappointments. In spite of all their prayer and concern they had a few failures both with staff and children—but they were comparatively few. The occasional unruly child had to be expelled as being uncontrollable, and now and then a member of staff had to be replaced after proving unsuitable. Even then God sometimes intervened at the last minute as in the case of one boy who was being dismissed for long standing bad conduct. Müller placed his hand upon the boy's head and began to pray for him. The young rebel would not close his eyes to pray but was determined to brazen it out to the bitter end. As he turned to stare defiantly at George Müller he was amazed to see the tears rolling down Müller's cheeks. The boy was converted on the spot and his life showed the change that had taken place.

Müller's supreme desire was always for the salvation of the orphans under his care, and over the years the great majority of them responded. Even some of the ones who left unconverted (and sometimes with a chip on their shoulder about the discipline in the orphanage—which was quite strict)—found they could not escape the prayers that were still offered up for them, and eventually they yielded their lives to Christ.

The homes were subject to problems common to bringing up children, such as the usual ailments and infectious diseases, except that their large numbers accentuated the dangers. During 1865 and 1866 there was an outbreak of scarlet fever: thirty-nine children went down with it but all recovered. There was also an outbreak of whooping-cough in the city of Bristol around this time and it was widespread and particularly virulent. It was an anxious time but there were only seventeen cases in Müller's homes and only one fatality.

There were occasions around this time when the Spirit of God swept through the homes in almost revival power. (The country was still enjoying the aftermath of the great 1859 revival.) One year there was a special visitation of God among the boys; another year the girls were especially affected and over a hundred of them entered into a real experience of salvation. Müller and his staff prayed that still more of the children would know and experience the power of God in their lives. It came about in an unusual way. A girl of seventeen, called Emma Bunn, who had been in the orphanage for fourteen years, was struck down with tuberculosis. Emma had always been something of a rebel and openly resisted the Christian teaching she received. Special prayer was now made for her in her dying condition, and the miracle happened— physically she was still terminally ill, but spiritually she was transformed. The change was so dramatic, Christ was now so real to her, that the news spread throughout the homes, resulting in a glorious work of grace taking place in what was tantamount to a small revival. In one home alone 350 were soundly and lastingly converted.

Müller's faith continued to grow and he was soon thinking about doubling their capacity to two thousand. Building costs were rising all the time but in 1869 he was able to open Number Four Home for boys, and in 1870 Number Five Home for girls. It was a colossal undertaking and the magnificent purpose-built, stone buildings, which dominated that area of the Ashley Downs were a tangible testimony to the power of prayer and faith in the Living God.

George prayed about everything—great and small. If he lost a key he made it a matter of prayer; when an appointment was not kept by someone, that became an occasion for prayer; if he came across a passage of Scripture which puzzled him he prayed for enlightenment; always he expected an answer. If it did not come immediately then he was prepared to wait patiently assured that in God's time he would receive a definite answer. Once he had discovered the will of God on a matter then he prayed and was confident of the response. In December, 1857, the boiler which heated the home started leaking badly; and it became apparent that a major repair was needed. The cold winter weather had set in and to be without heat for any length of time would cause suffering from the cold for the children. George knew that to pray without taking practical steps to replace the boiler would be presumption not faith. He prayed specifically for two things: first, that the Lord would change the cold north wind into a south wind; and second, that He would give the workmen a mind to work. The evening before the appointed day for the repair the bleak north wind was still blowing, but next day the south wind blew instead. The workmen of their own accord volunteered to work all night and the job was completed in thirty hours and the fire relit in the boiler. All that time the south wind blew so mildly that there was no need for a fire.

In January 1865 there was a tremendous gale in the Bristol area and the roofs of the orphan houses were badly damaged and many windows broken. It was Saturday which meant that no work could commence until Monday. Müller lifted up his heart to God and asked Him to change the weather until the repairs could be affected—otherwise with so many slates and windows missing they would suffer much more damage. The weather duly changed and the rain kept off until the following Wednesday, when a heavy rain shower drove the slaters off the roof. One part was still badly exposed and the rain threatened to cause serious damage. Immediately Müller prayed that the rain would cease until the work was finished. The rain duly obliged—and due to the direction of the wind it was found that because the hole was on the opposite side of the roof, the rain had not caused any further damage. The roofers returned and the repairs were completed.

All through these busy years, George Müller was faithfully pastoring the growing work at Bethesda and Gideon Chapel with his friend Henry Craik. The work had grown to some seven hundred strong and was becoming known as an important centre of the new Brethren Movement. During an unfortunate division which developed in the movement during the 1830s and 1840s, George Müller's pastoral care was tested to its fullest—and found not wanting. Müller and Craik came through unscathed by a bitter controversy with J.N. Darby, (the champion of Exclusive Brethrenism) and the flock under their watchful shepherding emerged virtually intact—to become the great rallying point of Open Brethrenism. In 1848 J.N. Darby went so far as to excommunicate Bethesda 'en bloc'. Müller never compromised his convictions concerning the truths of God's Word as he understood them, but he refused to be cramped by any narrow sectarianism and his heart remained wide open to all true believers everywhere.

In 1866 Müller lost his closest friend and colleague, when Henry Craik died. They had laboured together in Bristol for thirty-four fruitful years. In 1870, about a month after the opening of the Number Five Home, Müller suffered an even greater loss in the death of his faithful and greatly loved wife Mary. It had been a near perfect marriage and they were in love to the end. Within a few hours of her passing Müller was found as usual at the Monday evening prayer meeting at Bethesda, where he asked his friends to praise God with him for such a life, and to pray 'that the Lord will so enable me to have fellowship in her joy that my bereaved heart may be occupied with her blessedness instead of my unspeakable loss'.

Both in the homes and in the church, Müller was able to do so much because he had gathered around him faithful workers who shared the burdens. Almost two years after the loss of his first wife, after much prayer, he decided that it was right for him to marry again, and at the end of November 1871, he married Miss Susannah Grace Sangar. He had known her for some twenty-five years and she was a worthy helper. He also felt that the time had come for him to appoint a successor to superintend the orphanages and in a man by the name of James Wright he was certain that he had found the man of God's choice. James Wright married Mr Müller's faithful and godly daughter Lydia, on November 16th, 1871. Lydia remained very close to her father and was also a woman of prayer.

In 1875, at the age of seventy, George Müller felt that God was clearly leading him to a worldwide ministry in which he was to share his faith and promote brotherly love among all true believers. Over the next seventeen years he travelled some two hundred thousand miles (before the days of air travel!) and preached in forty-two different countries. Everywhere his ministry was tremendously appreciated; Müller had become a world figure and Christians flocked to hear him. His growing fame did not, strangely enough, bring with it an automatic increase in giving for the great work of SKI: Müller still found that he had to 'pray in' the support for SKI in its many activities, including the orphanges. Right to the end of his days, his faith was being developed by further tests, but Müller cheerfully accepted the discipline of his Heavenly Father without murmuring or questioning. Always he refused to go into debt, and when necessary he was willing to sell ten acres of land which was no longer absolutely essential for their requirements, to relieve their difficult financial situation. The testing lasted several years (by which time George was in his late eighties)—until in 1894 they emerged once more into a time of God's abundance.

In his ninetieth year Müller suffered the loss of his second wife who had been such a comfort to him and a faithful companion during their world travels. His mind was still clear and his faith undimmed and he continued to preach and be very active to the end of his long and fruitful life. In the last year of his life he wrote that his faith had been increasing, little by little, for sixty-nine years, but he insisted that there was nothing unique about him or his faith—such a life of trust was open to all God's children if only they would endure when trials came instead of giving up. He revealed that on his prayer list were the names of some for whom he had prayed for over sixty years for their salvation. He believed that God would answer his prayers and that he would see them in heaven. Other individuals on his prayer list had yielded to Christ one after another over the course of the years in which he resolutely remembered them in prayer every day of his life, wherever he was and however busy he was. One man was converted after eighteen months; another after five years; another after eleven years. Of the two for whom he prayed for over sixty years, one became a Christian just before Müller's death and the other a few years later.

On the evening of March 9th, 1898, George led the evening prayer meeting at Ashley Down and then retired for the night. In the morning he awoke early as usual and dressed himself ready for his quiet time but that morning the King of kings, in whose presence he had spent so much time in prayer, called him home to heaven. His funeral was one of the greatest that Bristol had ever witnessed as tens of thousands lined the streets to honour the foreigner who had become her most famous son—and whose name is forever linked with the city.

After his death his son-in-law and successor, James Wright, disclosed that the mysterious name of a generous donor which had appeared on the Annual Reports for many years as 'from a servant of the Lord Jesus who, constrained by the love of Christ, seeks to lay up treasurer in heaven', was none other than George Müller himself. The amounts given by him personally reached the staggering total (for those days) of

£81,490. Müller was a faithful giver as well as a faithful prayer warrior. This was all given out of his own money—money given to him for his own use or left to him personally in legacies. It was his lifelong practice to live very simply and carefully and to give all that was left after those basic needs had been met. He never stored up wealth for himself, not even as a pension; he constantly gave all, believing that God would continue to meet his every need even in old age. His entire personal estate at his death amounted to only £169, which included books, furniture, and personal items to the value of over £100, with only just over £60 in cash.

Under the banner of SKI so much had been achieved besides the orphanages. Through SKI Müller had been able to give 122,683 pupils a Christian education. He had been able to distribute over a quarter of a million Bibles and almost one and a half million New Testaments. Hundreds of missionaries had been supported to the tune of over a quarter of a million pounds. In all he had received for the work under the umbrella of the Scriptural Knowledge Institute £1,424,646. This sum was the grand total of the monies received and distributed for the orphanages, schools, missionaries, scriptures and Christian literature. He had cared for over ten thousand orphans.

George Müller's formula was basically very simple, 'A little more prayer, a little more faith, a little more patience, and the answer is sure to come'.

2: Hudson Taylor

It was a proud Sunday for the Methodists crowded in Barnsley Wesleyan Chapel in 1832; they all felt they were sharing the joy of James and Amelia Taylor in the christening of their first baby, James Hudson. James Taylor owned a chemist's shop in the town and also had a reputation as a gifted local preacher in the Methodist churches around the area. As this stockily built figure stood before the congregation, it was clear to all that he was taking this very seriously, in keeping with his solemn and strict character. During the long winter months when his young wife was pregnant, he had shared some Bible verses in Exodus and Numbers with her which had deeply impressed him, about all the firstborn belonging very specially to the Lord. After long and earnest discussion they had knelt together to set apart for the Lord the little life being formed in Amelia's womb. Now as she stood beside her resolute husband, holding in her arms their beautiful but oh so delicate little son, she bubbled with joy. Amelia (née Hudson) was the talented and attractive daughter of the minister of the church. She had a beautiful singing voice and possessed her father's irrepressible sense of humour—making her an ideal counter-balancing companion for James.

The name of Taylor was especially honoured among Barnsley Methodists. Grandfather James Taylor and his wife Betty were the pioneers of Methodism in Barnsley. In their home at the top of Old Mill Lane they had started the first Methodist Class Meeting in the town, and the first Methodist 'Church in the House' gathered there for worship. The great

John Wesley himself had visited their humble cottage.

As the congregation dispersed after the christening, stories of those heroic pioneer days were revived. 'Grandfather Taylor were afraid o' nowt and nobody. 'E were a real 'ero. Tha's got sommat to be proud of belonging to this chapel—and dinna thee forget it,' proud Yorkshire fathers told their sons and daughters, in their broad dialect. It had cost something to be a Methodist in those early days. Grandfather Taylor had been stoned, dragged in the dirt, manhandled and his life endangered, but he had never wavered in openly testifying for Christ. On one occasion powdered glass was rubbed in his eyes, but James and Betty Taylor prayed for those who treated them spitefully; God honoured their witness, and the cottage became a recognised centre of blessing. Though poor they tithed their income faithfully and the work prospered so that before his early death, Grandfather Taylor had the joy of seeing the first Wesleyan Chapel opened in Barnsley.

Young James Hudson Taylor has certainly got a name to live up to, folk said. But some of those shrewd Yorkshire women in their local gossip voiced their doubts about the little mite ever growing up—'he looks so pale and delicate, poor thing,' they said among themselves. But prayer changes things and that frail baby born on the 21st May 1832 was destined to become one of the greatest missionaries of all time.

Living behind the chemist's shop had its compensations—it meant that the children (four others were added to the Taylor family) saw plenty of their father. James Taylor was a very devout Christian and a good father, though rather too strict at times. Fortunately this tendency to over sternness was balanced by his wife Amelia's gentler care for the growing family. James Taylor expected a lot of his children, sometimes too much. By the time young Hudson was four his father had taught him the Hebrew alphabet. Not only did they have family prayers and Bible reading every morning and evening, but James Taylor took his children with him when he shut himself in his room to pray in secret. Little Hudson learned very early in life about the reality of prayer and the presence of God.

The Taylors were blessed with five children in all: James Hudson, William Shepherd, Amelia Hudson, Theodore and Louise Shepherd in that order. Sadly both Hudson's brothers died very young, which only served to show how remarkable it was that Hudson survived. In his infancy he was too delicate to go to school, though he was bright and quick to learn. They were able to afford a maid which enabled Amelia to devote time to teaching her children. Amelia was educated at the Friends' School in Darlington, and had experience as a governess to a gentleman-farmer's family. She was an excellent teacher and especially good at English which ensured that her children received a very good foundation for their learning. They soon acquired healthy appetites for reading, which led on to a love of literature, history and—through travellers' stories—a knowledge of geography and the world at large, including the mysterious land of China. Five year old Hudson was heard to say more than once, 'When I am a man I will be a missionary and go to China.'

Hudson was seven years old when Methodism celebrated its centenary and Barnsley and other parts of Yorkshire experienced a real breath of revival blessing. James Taylor had a class of nearly fifty boys and Amelia had a number of girls under her care; during the revival many of these young people were soundly converted and the Taylors' cup of joy overflowed. Young though he was, those days of revival left a lasting impression upon Hudson.

At eleven years of age Hudson's parents felt that his health had improved enough to venture sending him to school. He worked hard at his studies but he was far from strong and almost every week had to have a day or two off for illness. Hudson's ambition to be a missionary to China persisted, but his parents abandoned their hopes of this coming to pass due to his poor health. It was a hard pill for his chemist father to swallow having originally had ambitions to go to China himself. When forced to abandon them, he had prayed that if God ever gave him a son, that son would become a missionary to China. (James Taylor never told Hudson about this prayer until seven years after his arrival in China.)

Just before Christmas, 1845, when he was thirteen, it was decided that it would be better for Hudson to carry on his studies at home and help his father in the shop. This pleased and suited him; he was very affectionate and his mother was able to see to it that with his learning he also received lots of love and laughter. This developed Hudson's inherent sense of humour—an invaluable quality which never deserted him to the end of his days.

James Taylor was a good man basically, but inclined to be somewhat overbearing and rather pompous. Whilst generous to the poor he was tight-fisted with his own. Hudson though small of build was growing up rapidly and making an attractive boy with his sandy-coloured curly hair, grey-blue eyes and straight nose. Being full of fun he began to find the strong religious atmosphere at home repressive, so he was not sorry when at fifteen years of age he was given the opportunity to work in a local bank. His lively sense of humour made him popular and before long he began to doubt his religious upbringing. He struggled for a time but he was no match for his sceptical fellow clerks, who mocked his religious narrowness and 'old-fashioned notions'. Very soon their cynicism rubbed off on to Hudson, as did their bad language. He began to develop new ideas about life and dreamed of wealth and fine things such as a big house and a horse to go hunting with some of his new companions. His mother wept over the change she saw taking place in him, and his father physically chastised him for swearing. But in any case Hudson's health could not stand up to the winter months and the gaslight brought on severe eyestrain through the close work he had to do in the bank. The result was that after less than a year he was back in his father's shop among the captivating assortment of coloured bottles and boxes of powders associated with a pharmacist.

Those mid-teen years were difficult for Hudson and his family. His changed attitude upset the household and the only person he felt able to talk to was his young thirteen-year-old sister Amelia. His unhappiness so affected her that she determined to pray for him three times every day until he was truly converted. She did not have long to wait.

Two or three weeks after Hudson's seventeenth birthday, his mother went to stay for two weeks with friends some seventy miles away. She too had been praying much for her son, and one afternoon after lunch, finding herself free, she went to her room, locked the door and got down on her knees to pray for Hudson's complete conversion, determined not to cease praying until she received an assurance that her request was granted. The hours passed and still she prayed until at last she could pray no more. She felt a witness of the Holy Spirit that her request was granted and that her son's salvation was already a reality.

That same afternoon, back at home, Hudson was having a half-day holiday. Finding himself with time on his hands and bored he went into his father's study to find a book to read. Failing to find one that interested him he flipped through a little pile of pamphlets. A gospel booklet attracted his attention and he picked it up but only with the intention of reading the story part. It was a warm June day and he retreated with it into the old warehouse behind the shop and curled up in a corner, fully intending to stop reading when he came to the religious bit. But one sentence suddenly struck him and made him think. The phrase was, 'The finished work of Christ'. Immediately the words 'It is finished' came into his mind. He had struggled to be a Christian in his own strength and failed; he had got the idea that one's bad deeds had to be somehow balanced or paid for by one's good deeds. Now the question came into his mind, 'What was finished?' Suddenly, like a light shining into his heart, the Holy Spirit revealed the truth to him. It was as clear and bright and warm as the rays of the summer sun shining outside. He realised that the debt of sin was paid in full by Christ for us, for the whole world. Then came the thought, If the whole work was finished and the whole debt paid, what was there left for him to do? The way of salvation dawned upon Hudson at that moment. He realised there was nothing to be done except to fall down on his knees and accept the Saviour and His salvation, and to praise Him for ever!

There and then he fell on his knees and was praising God. At that precise moment, many miles away his mother was also on her knees praising God for the assurance which had suddenly come to her that her prayers for Hudson's salvation had been answered.

It was several days before Hudson ventured to share his experience with anyone. The first to be told was his young sister Amelia, and then only after he had made her promise to keep it a secret. Several more days passed before his mother returned home and Hudson was bursting to tell her his good news. He met her at the door and said, 'Mother, I have some happy news for you.' She hugged him and surprised him by saying, 'I know, my boy; I have been rejoicing for days in the glad tidings you have to tell me.' Hudson was taken aback. 'Has my sister broken her promise then, and told you?' he asked. His mother assured him that nobody had told her anything, but God Himself had revealed it to her, and she related to her amazed son the story of her afternoon's praying. No wonder Hudson was convinced from the very time of his conversion in June 1849, of the power of prayer.

That summer was, on the whole for Hudson, a very happy and satisfying one as he experienced the first joys of salvation and service. He found courage to confess Christ to his friends, and started to distribute religious tracts and invite people to the services. Then, along with his young sister Amelia, he began 'door-knocking' in the poorest parts of the town, witnessing and giving out tracts.

In the autumn, however, a reaction set in, and throughout the next three months Hudson struggled with himself; feeling that he was not living up to the high standards expected of a real Christian. Some of his reproach was needless—he tried to suppress his lively sense of humour and love of boyish fun, feeling that he should be more serious. Another factor contributing to Hudson's depression was undoubtedly the first break in the family circle at that time when his sister Amelia went away to a girls' school in Barton-on-Humber.

On Sunday, 2nd December 1849, Hudson was confined to the house with a cold. He sat down to write a long letter to Amelia whom he was still missing terribly. He wrote, 'Pray for me, dear Amelia, pray for me. I am seeking entire sanctification. Oh, that I could take hold of the blessed promises of God's Holy Word. My heart longs for perfect holiness'. But he finished on a very depressing note: 'I cannot help wishing that instead of a slight cold I had some sickness that would take me to Heaven'.

That night on his knees at his bedside Hudson wrestled with God, crying for His help. If only God would answer his prayer and save him completely and keep him from falling, he would go anywhere, do anything. He surrendered himself absolutely to the Lord and dedicated his life to God's service. It was a sacred moment and one of which he rarely spoke but he once wrote of it: 'Never shall I forget the feeling that came over me then. Words can never describe it. I felt I was in the presence of God, entering into covenant with the Almighty. I felt as though I wished to withdraw my promise, but could not. Something seemed to say, "Your prayer is answered, your conditions are accepted" '.

Then as clearly as if a voice had spoken, in his heart he heard the command, 'Then go for Me to China'. From that moment his mind was made up: with an almost frightening determination Hudson set himself to go to China. Late though it was, he could not resist opening the letter to his sister and penning a postscript with the glad news that Christ had revealed Himself to him most wonderfully. 'I cannot write for joy,' he said.

From that moment China was burned indelibly on his soul. Very little was known about that great and mysterious land at that time and books about China were very few. However, the Sunday school superintendent, Mr Whitworth, had recently become connected with the British and Foreign Bible Society and Hudson was able to obtain from him a copy of Luke's gospel in Mandarin. Unable to afford a Chinese grammar or dictionary, he set himself the task of mastering as many Chinese characters as possible. He started getting up at 5 am determined not only to pray but to study to prepare himself for China, by brushing up his Latin, and mastering the rudiments of Greek and Hebrew.

Discovering that the local Congregational minister had a copy of a book on China by Dr Medhurst of the London Missionary Society, Hudson went to the manse and asked if he could borrow it, explaining that God had called him to be a missionary to China. 'And how do you propose to go there?' asked the minister. Hudson replied that he would probably have to trust the Lord as much as the twelve apostles had done when sent out by Jesus. The minister smiled at such boyish naivety—Hudson being small looked even younger than his seventeen years—and placing his hand kindly on him he said, 'As you grow older you will become wiser than that.' (When Hudson was much older he said, 'I have grown older but not wiser. I am more convinced than ever that if we took the Master's directions to His disciples, we should find them just as suited today!')

Returning with the precious volume by Medhurst, Hudson eagerly devoured it, along with every scrap of information about China he could lay his hands on. The thought of China's four hundred million people in almost total ignorance of the gospel of Christ weighed heavily about him. At all costs he must prepare himself for his missionary calling. To toughen himself he made physical exercise a regular discipline, taking long walks over the moors. He also gave up sleeping in his soft featherbed and adopted a more spartan resting place.

One day, a new magazine called *The Gleaner* came into his hands. It was published by The Chinese Association, later renamed The Chinese Evangelization Society. This was undenominational and owed its existence mainly to the tremendous zeal and energy of a German called Dr Karl Gutzlaff, a most brilliant man with many gifts and talents although, as was later proved, wisdom, discretion and sound judgment were sadly not among them. Nevertheless he was instrumental in bringing the claims of China's millions before Europe in a startling and dramatic way.

Hudson was thrilled and inspired by Gutzlaff's achievements and exploits. As interpreter for the British government in Hong Kong, Gutzlaff was in a position of influence, and with almost reckless daring he had made many journeys into inland China in the 1830's. He translated the Scriptures into Chinese and founded The Chinese Union with the aim of using Chinese converts to evangelise their own land. The results were apparently spectacular, Gutzlaff's Chinese workers reporting nearly three thousand converts.

Prior to this Hudson had wondered how he could ever reach China. The Methodists had no work there and an early and boyishly immature letter he had written to the London Missionary Society had not even been acknowledged. It was an unsettling period in very many ways. His father had clashed with the Barnsley Methodist leaders and had joined the reformed breakaway group which became known as the Methodist Free Church. Hudson began his fellowship among the Plymouth Brethren, who were a source of inspiration to him. But the most unsettling factor during this crucial time in his life was a young schoolfriend brought home for the holidays by his sister Amelia. Young Hudson was well and truly smitten by the many charms of this attractive young lady, Miss Vaughan, a music teacher. He came under her spell but the question which nagged him over many months was 'would she be willing to go to China?'

Shortly after his eighteenth birthday Hudson started corresponding with George Pearse in London, who was the secretary of the Chinese Evangelization Society. Thanks to the efforts of Dr Gutzlaff and his tour through Europe, which included a visit to London, people in Britain had begun to support the work. Hudson started sending money to the Society, the founders of which were mostly Brethren business-men with an international and interdenominational vision. They were very sincere but seemed to leave their business acumen behind them when it came to the practicalities of missionary work.

Hudson began to feel his need for wider experience and he prayed about the matter. He had been with his chemist father for over four years and had gained invaluable experience and training in pharmacy. His prayers were soon answered, for the way opened for him to receive medical training from a relative, Dr Robert Hardey, who was a doctor in Hull. The doctor lectured in a local medical school as well as having a large general practice. Eighteen year old Hudson was made dispenser to Dr Hardey and the medical training and spiritual testings he received at this time were an ideal proving ground for the would-be missionary.

Meanwhile, just across the River Humber Hudson's sister Amelia was studying and his new sweetheart, Miss Vaughan, was teaching. Their love for each other blossomed and Hudson was completely infatuated. He kept the ferry busy and cherished the times they spent around the piano when she dazzled him with her talented playing and singing and occasionally Hudson joined her in singing a duet. But under-neath the charm, Miss Vaughan was firmly resolved not to go to China and confident she could woo Hudson away from his 'stupid' missionary notions. Hudson was just as confident that he could win her round to his way of thinking and equally resolved to go to China.

At first Hudson lived with Dr Hardey, then with an aunt;

but he felt the need to prove God for himself if he was to survive once he was thousands of miles away from home in China. He eventually found a bed sit in one of the poorest parts of Hull called Drainside, choosing it in order to live as cheaply as possible and to give away two-thirds of his income. His diet was homely and simple but he was happy and content. This was not the case with Miss Vaughan, however. Visiting Hudson in this slum area proved too much for her fine sensibilities and Hudson was soon forced to face up to the fact he would lose her friendship if he persisted on his present course. He was extremely depressed at the prospect but came through the trial chastened, stronger and more determined.

Hudson spent his spare time working among the poor of the neighbourhood, giving what practical and medical help he could as well as distributing tracts. Fellowship with the Plymouth Brethren in Hull stimulated his growing love for the Word of God, and regular news through their ranks of such noted Brethren as George Müller increased his faith in the power of God to provide for every need. Soon he was writing to his mother, 'I feel as if I could not live if something is not done for China'. He felt that he must put to the test his belief that it was possible to move man through God by prayer alone. After some thought he decided on his course of action. Dr Hardey, being a very busy man, left it to Hudson to remind him whenever his salary was due. Hudson determined that he would not do this verbally but simply pray about it. His salary was paid quarterly and as the time for its payment came round Hudson made it a matter of special prayer. Several days passed and the good doctor said not a word about the overdue salary. Hudson found himself at the end of the week with only one half-crown coin (eight such coins made one pound).

On Sunday morning he worshipped happily with his friends and then spent the afternoon and evening visiting and witnessing among the poor. At ten o'clock that night on his way home an Irishman asked him if he would accompany him home to pray with his wife who was dying after having given birth to a baby only the day before. Hudson found himself in an overcrowded squalid little room where the dying mother was lying on a mattress with her two-day-old baby whimpering beside her, and several more children standing around. A battle raged in Hudson's young mind: if only his money was in several lesser coins, then he would gladly have given them most of it, but the thought of emptying his pocket completely and leaving himself penniless was just too much. He tried to pray but the words almost choked him and an inner voice told him he was a hypocrite. The man pleaded with him to help them get some milk and food if he possibly could. Still Hudson hesitated; slowly he put his hand in his pocket and felt the precious coin. Then in a moment the battle was won; he handed it to the man with a blessing and a word of testimony and immediately his joy returned. Through it the woman's life was eventually spared as the thankful man went to procure supplies of food (quite a lot could be bought for that amount in those days).

Hudson's heart was light as he returned through the dark deserted streets to his own humble home. He could not resist bursting out into songs of joyous praise to God. He had taken a small but most important step of faith, as significant as when a first time swimmer takes his feet off the bottom and launches out to swim a few strokes. However, the thing that had worried him was the fact that he had no food in prospect for lunch the next day as he was still determined not to remind the doctor about his overdue salary, and rely instead on God answering his prayers. True, it was only like learning to swim in the local swimming pool with a life-belt always in reach, but if he could not keep above water in that, he would certainly never survive in the ocean. But for the moment tomorrow could take care of itself. He was as happy as a prince, he had sufficient thin porridge for supper that night and his breakfast in the morning. As he knelt to pray he reminded the Lord of the promise in His Word, 'He that giveth to the poor lendeth to the Lord'; and with unaffected naivety he asked the Lord not to let the loan be a long one or he would have no dinner tomorrow!

Next morning Hudson was just finishing the last of his porridge for breakfast when the postman came with a letter. It was unusual for him to receive mail on Mondays; he did not recognise the handwriting and with some excitement he opened it. Inside was a pair of kid gloves and a gold half-a-sovereign (with a value of ten shillings or the equivalent of four half-crowns). The significance of this was not lost upon Hudson and he burst out spontaneously, 'Praise the Lord, four hundred per cent for twelve hours' investment—that is good interest! What bank would not jump at the chance to lend money at such a rate of interest!' There and then he determined that God henceforth should be his banker. It was a test case which served to strengthen his faith for the rest of his life.

However, the story was still incomplete; there remained the matter of his unpaid salary. One week passed, then two and the doctor's amnesia remained, but the half-sovereign Hudson had received through the post was now spent. He intensified his praying, feeling the battle was not so much over the money but rather over the whole question of whether he could go to China on the strength of prayer alone. At the end of the second week he was facing the embarrassment of being unable to pay his landlady. What should he do? Should he ask the doctor?—it would be such a simple thing. He asked God for guidance and felt that he should learn to wait God's time, and received an assurance that his Heavenly Father would undertake. Saturday evening came and at 5 pm he was with the doctor helping in the surgery when suddenly Dr Hardey said, 'By-the-way, Taylor isn't your salary due?' Hudson was delighted but his joy was short lived as the doctor, after expressing his regrets for forgetting the overdue salary, apologised that he could not pay at that moment having sent all his ready cash to the bank that very afternoon. Hudson's heart was plunged into the depths again. When he was alone he poured out his heart to God for help, and his peace was restored together with a conviction that he would see God's hand in the matter.

Hudson remained at the doctor's surgery until 10 pm and was just preparing to leave for his lodging without the money to pay his landlady, disappointed that it would now be Monday before anything could be done, when Dr Hardey came into the surgery again—laughing heartily. It transpired that one of his richest patients had inexplicably called to pay his bill in cash late at night, when he could have settled it by cheque at his own convenience. The doctor then used the money to pay Hudson his salary—and only then did Hudson realise that in this way God was showing him that He could move the hearts of men to do His bidding. Hudson with a joyful heart realised that after all he could go to China—trusting only in the Lord.

During this period in Hull Hudson was growing and maturing spiritually; his fellowship with such gifted Brethren leaders as Andrew Jukes enriched his life greatly and increased his appreciation of the Word of God. This was just as well because a number of disappointments and tests also came into his life. It took him a long time to get over his broken friendship with Miss Vaughan. Then his father wanted Hudson to come home and mind the business for two years whilst he went on a protracted business trip to Canada and America to explore the possibilities in those new and growing countries. Hudson was shattered and rebelled bitterly at first but finally he submitted and expressed his willingness, even though it meant further delay in his own preparations to go to China. As it happened his father abandoned the idea. Then it was established that growing rumours about Dr Gutzlaff's work proved all too true. The sensational results which he had claimed for his Chinese workers and which had thrilled so many—and young Hudson especially—proved to be entirely false. Gutzlaff himself had been deceived by his Chinese agents who had concocted most of their colourful reports.

The revelation completely shattered Gutzlaff and within a few months he died a broken-hearted man on August 9th 1851 after a brief illness in Hong Kong. He was only forty-eight years of age. His supporters mostly evaporated away at the disclosures but Gutzlaff's labours were not entirely in vain. In later years Hudson Taylor credited him as being the grandfather of the China Inland Mission.

In spite of everything, Hudson was still totally obsessed with China and when news came of the impending visit to London of another German missionary to China, called Mr Lobscheid, he determined to meet him if at all possible. The way opened up for him to visit London with his young sister Amelia, and it proved to be a highlight in both of their lives. Not that Mr Lobscheid himself was very encouraging to Hudson; he told him that his light-coloured hair and grey-blue eyes would be a distinct disadvantage to his acceptance by the Chinese. But God was bringing Hudson into contact with people who were to prove to be his life-long friends and staunch supporters. He met George Pearse, the secretary of the Chinese Evangelization Society, who introduced him to a group of Christians at Bruce Grove, Tottenham, who regularly interceded for China.

This visit to the capital made it apparent to Hudson that his next step in his preparations must be to move to London. He gave in his notice to Dr Hardey in August 1852 and prayed that God would open the way for him to continue his training in London. An uncle offered him accommodation and the Chinese Evangelization Society offered to pay his hospital fees for training at the Ophthalmic Hospital and a course at the London Hospital. He still needed a position to complete the picture, but he believed that God would undertake and so it was that at just over twenty years of age, he arrived in London on September 25th 1852.

Hudson immediately turned this into another adventure of faith. His father had offered to bear all his expenses whilst in London, and the Chinese Evangelization Society had done the same. As he prayed over the matter he saw that this presented him with an ideal opportunity to prove God's faithfulness. He decided to write to both of them declining their kind offers; he did so realising that as they both had been told of the other's offer, each would think that he had accepted the support of the other! This would therefore leave him entirely free to trust God without anyone knowing.

Life in the great metropolis came as quite a shock to Hudson after the comparative slowness and smallness of Barnsley and Hull. In London everything was hustle and bustle and he felt very small and more than a little lonely. His uncle, true to his promise, provided accommodation in the same boarding house as himself and a cousin of Hudson's, Tom Hudson, very kindly gave him the chance to share his attic room in the same establishment, which was a considerable saving financially.

Hudson's funds were very limited but his confidence was unlimited. When his uncle and Tom asked him about his plans his replies baffled them and ultimately began to annoy them. He told them he did not want to take a regular apprenticeship because he did not want to bind himself for a long period of time: he wanted to be free to go to China as soon as possible, and God would undertake for him! But the path of true faith, like true love, never runs smoothly. His first rude shock came when he learned from the office of the Chinese Evangelization Society that they had not yet made definite arrangements for him to begin work at the hospital—they had been waiting for him to arrive first! He was beginning to learn about the way committees work—or don't work. At the earliest it would be three or four weeks before he could start—and first there was much paperwork to be attended to. Meanwhile he continued with his own studies in the attic bedroom, as well as wrestling with the problems of how to stretch his funds to the utmost by living as frugally as possible. His diet was ridiculously simple, consisting of a large brown loaf, apples and water. This meant he could subsist on one pound for about two months—so far as food was concerned.

A month after arriving in London Hudson at last started at the London Hospital. As this was four miles from his lodgings, and he could not afford the bus fares of six pence a day, he walked there and back, making eight miles a day— through often foggy streets by the river, and on a far from full stomach. He was happy and content but the strain of such an inadequate diet and lifestyle took its toll.

Out of the kindness of his heart Hudson undertook a little task for his landlady in Hull. Her husband was a seaman and to save her paying the commission on this monthly payment, Hudson offered to collect the money from the shipping office near Cheapside, and forward it to her, which he did faithfully. One month, however, he was busy with examinations and he forwarded the money out of his own pocket. When he did find time to call at the shipping office he was informed that the man's pay had been stopped as he had left the ship and gone to the gold diggings! Hudson was devastated, knowing that there was no way could he write to the dear lady and ask her to return the money he had sent her out of his own pocket. It was a severe blow to his already depleted funds.

To top it all, whilst engaged at the hospital in dissecting the body of a man who had died from a deadly fever, Hudson contracted blood poisoning. Before the end of the day he was feeling desperately ill. When he spoke to the surgeon in charge it transpired that he had obviously picked up the infection through a prick in his finger. The surgeon said, 'You are a dead man—get home as quickly as possible'. Hudson could not afford to take a cab home and started to walk, feeling worse with every step. In the end he was compelled to take a bus and somehow he struggled back to his lodgings. For weeks his life was in the balance but slowly he began to recover. His doctor urged him to go home to Barnsley for a rest but he had no money left for his fare and his family were unaware of what had happened because he'd remained silent for fear of worrying them.

What should he do in this predicament? As he prayerfully considered the situation the impression came into his mind that he should call again at the shipping office. It seemed useless, foolish even—to what purpose? Furthermore it was two miles to Cheapside and he had no money. He was too weak even to walk downstairs by himself, but the conviction was so strong that he determined he would at least try to walk there because he felt sure of the divine direction. By the time Hudson arrived at the shipping office he was so exhausted he had to sit on the steps before attempting to climb them. Once inside he found he was not mistaken about God's leading: the office had discovered they had made a mistake. The deserter was another man with the same name; the back pay and the current money were handed over to Hudson. He was able to send the remittance for the current month to his former landlady in Hull, and also reimburse himself for the money he had laid out from his own pocket and still had sufficient to pay his fare home to Barnsley.

Such experiences as these, coupled with Hudson's courage and faith, could not fail to impress and before long he had the unspeakable joy of pointing his room-companion, cousin Tom, to Christ. Once home it was impossible to keep from his family how he had been existing in London and his mother wisely forbade him to live like that again—his frail constitution would never have stood up to it.

When he returned to London in January 1853 Hudson secured a position as assistant to a surgeon at Bishopsgate, which gave him the double benefits of home comforts and being nearer to the hospital.

In the Spring of 1853 a revolution in China was making the headlines and The Times was calling it 'the greatest revolution ever.' Known as the Taiping (Great Peace) Rebellion, it had started under a Chinese who professed Christianity, called Hung Hsiu-ch'üan. Subsequently it degenerated into a corrupt political movement but at the time it seemed providential and the Chinese Evangelization Society saw it as the answer to their prayers. They immediately began to make plans to send someone out to China to capitalise on this promising situation. It was resolved to ask Hudson Taylor if he would be willing to go, and so it was that just two weeks after his twenty-first birthday, young Hudson found himself sooner than he had anticipated with the opportunity of going to his beloved China. Such was his eagerness he was willing to go without even going home again, but as it happened his departure could not be effected so speedily and he had time to visit the family in Barnsley before setting sail for China on September 19th, 1853, on the small sailing-ship, the 'Dumfries', from Liverpool. His mother came to see him off. It was a costly parting which left a deep mark upon both of them. After all, Hudston Taylor was just a little over twenty-one years of age, and the mysterious land of China was five and a half months away by sea. As Hudson waved his last farewell to his mother from the ship her anguished cry reached him and in that moment he began to understand in a new way the cost of his venture.

The ship had hardly embarked on its long journey before a tremendous storm hit them just of the Welsh coast and threatened to dash them to pieces on the rocks. The storm was ferocious and prolonged and for twelve days they never escaped from the channel. In the fearful battering of that awful storm Hudson learned another valuable lesson which stood him in good stead for the rest of his life. To please his mother he had obtained a life-belt, but it seemed inconsistent to him to trust in God and have a life-belt. When it seemed that there was no possible hope of surviving the storm and with things at their worst, he gave the life-belt away and immediately felt at peace. Nevertheless he made sure that he had something near at hand which would float if the ship was wrecked!

After the storm finally abated Hudson studied the question of God's provision, searching the Scriptures and praying the matter through. He came to the conclusion that it is not wrong to use the natural means God provides (from doctors to life-belts!) as ways out of troubling situations. He proved for himself that God can heal with or without means, but the guiding principle is to pray about all things and seek God's guidance and wisdom in every situation.

Once free from the storm and out into the ocean Hudson sought permission to conduct regular services for the crew (he was the only passenger). The captain gave his permission but although Hudson prepared his messages diligently and saturated them with prayer, he saw no visible results during the long voyage. There was, however, one striking answer to prayer which none of the crew could ever forget. When sailing to the north of New Guinea, they found that although a breeze would usually spring up after sundown and last until dawn, during the daytime they were frequently becalmed.

On this particular day the captain was clearly anxious, and when Hudson asked him what was troubling him, he explained that a strong under-current was carrying them towards some sunken reefs. The situation was fraught with danger. In an effort to turn the ship away from the shore the long-boat was launched but the task proved physically impossible. The captain said there was nothing more they could try, they could now only wait for the worst to happen. Up piped baby-faced Hudson: 'No, there is one thing we have not done yet—we have not prayed.'

There were three more committed Christians on the ship and Hudson suggested that the four of them should each retire to their own cabins and pray for the Lord to send a breeze immediately. The captain agreed and the four of them set themselves to pray. Hudson prayed for only a matter of minutes before he felt an assurance that their prayers were answered. Without further ado he went up on deck and asked the first officer (a rank unbeliever) to set the sail to catch the coming wind. The man nearly exploded at such an apparently ridiculous suggestion—especially coming from this stripling of a landlubber, who, to cap this farcical nonsense, was religious. Hudson somehow persuaded him to try, confidently expressing his faith that God was sending them a wind. The situation had now become so dangerous that there was no time to lose—the reef was perilously close. Against his better judgment and with a curse in his mouth and contempt in his eyes, the first officer gave the order and the men jumped to obey. The commotion brought the captain up on deck to see what was happening. No sooner was the sail set than the prayer-answering breeze filled it and the ship was soon pulling away from the reef to the safety of the open sea. It was a great witness to all on board and a tremendous encouragement to Hudson's ever-increasing faith.

Over five months after leaving Liverpool they finally arrived in China, the ship moving slowly up a fog-bound river, and at 5 pm on Wednesday, 1st March 1854 Hudson was able to set foot on Chinese soil at Shanghai. It was a moment of great emotion for him, but his first moments of elation soon gave way to a feeling of great loneliness when he realised that there was not a single soul waiting to welcome him. He had three letters of introduction, but inquiries revealed that one of his contacts had died and another had left for America, leaving him with only one hope—Dr Medhurst of the London Missionary Society. He was immensely relieved to find that Dr Medhurst was still in Shanghai, but locating him proved difficult as the city was found to be in the hands of the rebels. A civil war was in progress with the troops of the Imperial army trying to oust the rebels. Everything was in a state of pure chaos: prices had rocketed, food was scarce and accommodation almost impossible to find in the war-torn city.

Other missionaries were kind to him but Hudson felt that he was an embarrassment to all concerned. His arrival at such a time seemed most inopportune. His funds were low and to make matters worse a remittance from the Chinese Evangelization Society in London, which should have been waiting for him on his arrival, had not been received. When eventually it did arrive it proved to be totally inadequate. It was a humiliating and inauspicious start to his missionary career. It soon became apparent that the C.E.S. back in London had not the remotest idea of the prevailing conditions in Shanghai and before long the Society's reputation in Shanghai was in tatters because of the way they treated this young missionary. Hudson's letters to them took an age to arrive and though he made the situation very plain they did nothing to alleviate his impossible situation.

Those first few months would have destroyed a lesser person. Because of the circumstances in which the C.E.S. had hurried Hudson out he had not been able to finish his medical training; he had a fair amount of experience but he lacked the vital qualifications: he was neither a doctor nor was he ordained. Nevertheless, he knuckled down to the study of the language in great earnest and did all and more than could reasonably have been expected of him. Somehow he struggled prayerfully and manfully through those nightmare months. The horrors of the siege, the abnormal conditions, the suffering, the brutalities he witnessed of the Chinese soldiers on both sides, all tested his resolve to the utmost. He did not lack courage and he used what medical knowledge and skill he possessed to alleviate the sufferings of the wounded. In spite of everything he was conscious of the presence of God in his life.

Hudson was learning missionary work the hard way but the difficult experiences he passed through during this period, largely due to the incompetence of the Society and their inadequate and irregular support, made him determined that he would do things differently if ever he was afforded the chance. From another source he suddenly learned that a missionary family had been sent from England by the Society: a medical man, Dr Parker, and his family. However, he did not receive word from the C.E.S. about their coming until they had arrived. Meanwhile Hudson continued his desperate search for accommodation and found some: it was poor and far from satisfactory but it was the best he could do with his lack of funds. Dr Parker arrived to find exactly the same situation as Hudson—the promised remittance from the C.E.S. in London had not been received.

The situation was farcical in the extreme yet somehow, in spite of it all, Hudson's humour did not entirely desert him and occasionally he still found the courage to laugh when there was precious little for him to laugh about. As he began to master the difficult language he was soon venturing forth on little evangelistic expeditions, giving out literature and seeking to win these suffering and lost Chinese people for his Saviour.

It was a year before a terrible battle at last brought a measure of peace to Shanghai. More than once Hudson's life was in danger during this period, but he was determined to venture inland as soon as there was an opportunity. All the starry-eyed notions of missionary work he had cherished back in Barnsley were well and truly dispelled by this time, but his contact with a raw heathenism which could kill new-born babies and throw them in the city drain without a qualm, and bind the feet of the women to produce tiny feet at the cost of terrible and senseless suffering, made him realise more than ever China's need of Christ. He was also disillusioned by the way some of the missionaries lived—it just did not fit in with his own deep convictions as to what a missionary should be.

Hudson himself tried living on a very simple diet of Chinese food but this was not suited to his far from robust constitution and his health suffered in consequence. At times the loneliness of being so far away from home overwhelmed him. In a letter home seeking to comfort a bereaved uncle, he wrote in July 1855, 'There are times when one feels most acutely what it is to be separated by 18,000 miles from all that is dear and beloved in this world. My position—one of peculiar loneliness and isolation—had let me feel something of the desolation which you have doubtless experienced'.

In spite of everything Hudson devoted himself faithfully to

mastering the difficult language, his one consuming passion to preach Christ where He had never been named before. Inland China drew him like a magnet. The new missionary, Dr Parker was a good man and because he was a fully qualified doctor he had a distinct advantage over young Hudson. They discovered once they ventured out of Shanghai and into the towns and cities whose inhabitants were not familiar with foreigners, that medicine was one marvellous means of overcoming the unreasonable fears of the Chinese.

For a time when Hudson was consumed with mastering the Chinese language his prayer life suffered and he realised that he was losing out spiritually. In England he had learned the value of spending the first hour of the day in prayer and communion with God. This became the resolute pattern of his life in China.

Soon with Dr Parker or other missionaries, and sometimes on his own, Hudson was making probing visits into areas rarely, if ever before, visited by missionaries. Some eight months after Dr Parker's arrival the opportunity was afforded Dr Parker of leaving Shanghai to open a hospital for the Chinese in Ningpo, and this left Hudson very much on his own once again.

For months the thought had been simmering in Hudson's mind that to reach the Chinese he must adopt Chinese dress all the time. This was an unheard of thing among European missionaries. Occasionally they would wear Chinese dress if travelling in the interior, but as soon as they were back in Shanghai they reverted to European dress. At the time of Dr Parker's departure for Ningpo to open the hospital, after weeks of searching and praying, Hudson suddenly found accommodation for himself in Shanghai—at a time when it was virtually unobtainable, especially at the price he could afford to pay. It was another wonderful answer to prayer which greatly encouraged him—and once having decided to 'go Chinese'—he needed all the encouragement he could get. He went all the way, not only wearing Chinese dress, but to the point of having his head shaved and the rest of his hair dyed black and a pigtail (or queue) plaited in with his own hair. Hudson found it easy to understand why the European community shunned him following this revolutionary step, but when the missionaries themselves also sneered at him, he found it very hard to bear.

Within three weeks of moving into his little house Hudson had the supreme joy of baptising his first convert in China. The young man, Kuei-hua, was the brother of a student Hudson was teaching. A few days later he was further encouraged when he received a letter from an interested supporter of his work, W. T. Berger, in which was enclosed a gift of £40. In view of the miserable failure of the Chinese Evangelization Society to provide him with regular and adequate support, this deepened his belief that should it come to it he could depend on God to supply his needs through prayer. To cap it all, there were one or two more promising inquirers after Christ; at last he began to feel that he was a real missionary.

Hudson had now been in China for almost two years, during which time he had been forced to contend with the civil war raging around him, the negligence of his Society in London, unkind and cruel criticisms from many quarters, and great loneliness. Nevertheless he had battled bravely through and things were beginning to change for the better. His heart was still set on moving inland, away from Shanghai and very wonderfully the opportunity came to him of renting a house on the populous island of Tsungming, some forty miles from Shanghai. From the moment of his arrival in Tsungming, Hudson found a ready response from these people when he set up a simple medical clinic for any needing treatment, and also began daily meetings where he talked about Christ. A few began to attend the meetings regularly and showed great interest in the message. Hudson met with the same welcome when, together with some helpers he ventured out into the many villages dotted thickly around the island. His medical treatment proved very successful with many who had suffered for years with what, for even his limited medical skill, were curable complaints. Unfortunately his success in this area was resented by the local quacks and they began complaining to the Mandarin and requesting him to remove the foreigners. It was an anxious time for Hudson as he had some promising young converts such as the blacksmith, Chang, and another young man called Sung, both of whom openly confessed their faith in Christ.

Just when it seemed their prayers were answered and the threatened expulsion by the Mandarin had been avoided, Hudson, during a short visit to Shanghai at the end of the year, found himself served with an official summons from the British Consul, to explain why he was residing outside the recognised five ports allowed by the British Treaty. The Consul instructed him to give up his house on the island at once, with the threat of a heavy fine of 500 dollars if he returned. It was a bitter blow and the only hope was for him to appeal to the Queen's representative, Sir John Bowring, who was expected shortly in Shanghai. His arrival was delayed, however, and in the interim God brought a key person into Hudson's life at this crucial time, in the form of William C. Burns, the outstanding Scottish revivalist.

William Burns had been greatly used by God in the famous 1839 Revival in Scotland as a consequence of which, although he was only a young man of twenty-four years at the time, he had rapidly become a household name throughout Scotland. Fortunately his deep devotion to Christ, and his love for souls, ensured that he remained unspoiled by such attention. He was a man of the Word and a mighty man of prayer. After preaching with great power and success in the North of England Burns had visited Canada, with equal blessing. In 1847 he sailed from England for China where he did out-standing missionary service in Canton and Amoy. He paid a brief visit home to Scotland in 1854 before returning to spend the rest of his days in China.

It was around the end of 1855, when Burns met poor Hudson who was then fretting and fuming over trying to prepare his case to Sir John Bowring for permission to stay on the Island. It was a providential meeting. Burns was by now a mature man of God and an experienced missionary. He quickly persuaded Hudson to drop the whole thing, to cease striving and accept it all as part of God's sovereign purposes. Hudson had heard of the reputation of this great Scottish revivalist and was a little afraid of him at first, but he quickly warmed to him and found his fears were groundless. Burns was seventeen years older than Hudson but the attraction was mutual; they were two kindred spirits. Both were men of prayer and faith with a burning passion to take the gospel to the Chinese in the remoter regions. The seven months in which they worked together were mutually beneficial. For Hudson the timing was perfect and he acknowledged that the help he received from Burns was crucial and of life long benefit.

They travelled by boats on the waterways around Shanghai for three months, preaching in the market-place and sharing the gospel at every opportunity. Between times Burns regaled Hudson with stirring stories of revival work and God's protection in the face of opposition in Dublin, Canada and Southern China. They talked about evangelism and the use of lay-evangelists as a lost order that Scripture required to be restored. These seed-thoughts blossomed later. Burns had proved from experience the value of quietly submitting himself to God in every trial, confident that God had a purpose which would ultimately turn out to be a blessing. It was a revelation to Hudson and brought a new rest of faith. However, as they went around together it was not lost on Burns that his young companion was more readily received in his Chinese dress than he was in his foreign attire. He was convinced it was the right thing to do and he changed into Chinese dress and never again reverted to European attire.

Through a Christian sea captain they heard about the great

spiritual need of a notorious place called Swatow, a port in the south of China, which was a centre of the opium trade and the dreadful coolie traffic. It was a place of violence and vice and without a missionary. Hudson felt the call of God to this place but was heartbroken because it seemed that it would spell the end of his friendship with Burns, whose companionship had come to mean so much to him. However, unknown to Hudson, God was also convicting Burns of the need to go to Swatow and Burns was dreading the prospect of telling Hudson! What joyous relief they experienced when they found that God was calling them *both* to Swatow.

The Christian sea captain offered them a free passage and so they left Shanghai on his steamer in March, 1856. For some four months during the almost unbearable heat of the tropical summer they laboured to make the gospel known in Swatow. Hudson was shocked with its wickedness which exceeded anything he had experienced. The Cantonese did not hide their hatred for these 'foreign pigs' but it was met in the spirit of Christ and with prayer. Hudson's medical skill was used to bring healing to an official whom the Chinese doctors had been unable to cure. As a consequence this official offered to rent them a house, something they had been desperately needing to enable them to start more effective and extensive medical work. Their lives were in constant danger because of the lawlessness that prevailed in and around Swatow, and through the frequent fighting between adjoining towns. However, they bravely persevered, witnessing wherever possible, and preaching at every opportunity, trusting God for their protection. Their results were encouraging as people began to respond to the gospel. Now that there was the prospect of renting the house for medical work, Hudson arranged to go to Shanghai to collect his medical equipment. A free passage was again offered him and though sorry to leave Burns even for a short time, he was looking forward to the short sea trip hoping that it would be a needed tonic to his health which was beginning to be badly affected by the heat and their poor living conditions.

Little did Hudson realise as he said goodbye to his dear friend Burns that he would never see him again. The clouds of war which were gathering over Southern China erupted violently following an incident involving the seizing by the Chinese of a ship flying a British flag which was smuggling opium. The whole affair was handled badly and the British began bombarding Canton. For four years Anglo-Chinese relations hit rock-bottom as hostilities flared up. Whilst Hudson was away, William Burns was seized as a prisoner and taken to Canton. Despite experiencing the wrath and foolishness of men, Burns proved the wisdom of quietly trusting God in every circumstance and he became trusted by friend and foe alike and known as 'The Man of the Book'. When he was eventually released he moved to Peking and ultimately to Manchuria. He finally ended his days preaching in the New Chang, where a short and sudden illness ended his outstanding life on April 4th, 1868.

Hudson Taylor, meanwhile, on his return to Shanghai was met with a whole series of disappointments. Firstly he found all his medical equipment had been destroyed in a fire. On his way to Ningpo to contact Dr Parker in the hope of obtaining medical supplies, his Chinese servant absconded with the baggage, leaving Hudson stranded. The events which followed were something of a nightmare. He was forced to seek to return to Shanghai; he was in no fit condition to make the journey alone and after a series of minor disasters Hudson fainted by the side of a canal. At last, however, help was forthcoming and he was eventually put on board a junk going towards Shanghai, although forced to complete the last part of his journey being carried in a Sedan chair.

However, it was in the midst of these apparent disasters that Hudson's fellowship with Burns really began to bear fruit, especially in the aspect of thinking of God as sovereign over every circumstance in our lives, both great and small. Instead of arriving back in Shanghai in a state of deep depression Hudson enjoyed a new experience of victory, this new encounter with his Saviour resulting in a renewed dedication.

Instead of prosecuting his thieving servant (whom he had been earnestly trying to win for Christ) Hudson decided to forgive him and wrote him a beautiful letter in which was mingled the right balance of mercy and warning. That settled, and physically recovered, he set out once more for Dr Parker in Ningpo and this time the journey was uneventful. At the time when it was most needed, another letter arrived from his faithful supporters Mr and Mrs Berger with a cheque for £40. God was proving His faithfulness and Hudson was learning fast that God's work done in God's way will never lack.

His letter home, telling about being robbed by his servant and his decision to forgive and not press charges, came in a round about way and through the providence of God into the hands of George Müller in Bristol. Müller was so impressed he immediately sent out a gift to cover Hudson's losses and became a faithful and increasingly generous supporter of his work.

Hudson stayed for several weeks helping Dr Parker in the growing medical work he was building up in Ningpo, but his heart was still in Swatow and as soon as possible he headed back to Shanghai with his replenished medical supplies. Several niggling delays occurred and he grew increasingly impatient but he discovered the hand of God was once again mysteriously at work. Just when he was ready to board the steamer for Swatow an urgent message reached him warning him not to go. Burns had been arrested and sent to Canton and the British authorities were not willing for Hudson to return in the present troubled circumstances. At first it was a bitter blow to him, but when news followed of the outbreak of hostilities with the British bombarding Canton and declaring war, he was thankful for everything which had held him back.

There was nothing for it but to return to Ningpo. There at long last, all lingering thoughts of his lost love back home in Hull were finally dispelled by a new vision of feminine loveliness with whom Hudson promptly fell deeply in love.

Maria Dyer and her older sister were teachers in the first girls' school opened by missionaries in China. Their parents had served as missionaries in China under the London Missionary Society. They had both died leaving their orphaned children to be brought up under the care of an uncle in London. The girls had returned to China to teach in the school run by a domineering and determined ageing spinster called Miss Aldersey. She was an outstanding personality in very many ways, having been the first unmarried woman missionary to go to China, and she ran an excellent school. Unfortunately for Hudson she took an instant dislike to him.

Although Hudson was immediately smitten by Maria (in spite of her slight squint in one eye), he kept his affections for her a secret for some weeks, hardly daring to hope that she would ever look at him. He was not the first to look wistfully in her direction, and two other hopefuls had got nowhere. Hudson watched and prayed and was increasingly attracted not only by her pleasing physical appearance and winsome nature but most of all by her spiritual keenness and desire to win souls. She was a kindred spirit.

After some months Hudson finally took his courage in his hands and wrote a letter to her expressing his feelings for her. He waited anxiously for the reply but when it came he was devastated. The reply was the very opposite of what he had hoped for—it was a total and absolute rebuttal. Unknown to him though Maria had penned the letter, it was the fearsome Miss Aldersey who had dictated it and virtually compelled her to write it. The truth was that Maria had a growing affection for Hudson but dared not go against Miss Aldersey.

It was a bitter trial for both of them but once again Hudson resorted to his unfailing weapon—prayer. As time passed he became convinced that she was the person for him and would make an ideal partner for his missionary work. Through this test, however, he learned the lesson of submitting his affections to the will of God. One book in the Bible in which he found new treasures was the Song of Solomon!

Hudson was also forced to face another great trial of faith. The Chinese Evangelization Society had been so unreliable in their support and on top of this he now learned that they were quite heavily in debt, a position which he deeply felt to be wrong for a Christian organisation. After just over three years in China he took the bold step of resigning his connection with the Society and determined in the future to trust God for his support. It was a momentous and courageous decision but one he never regretted. He was to demonstrate to the world the faithfulness of God.

Eventually Hudson learned the truth about the letter Maria had been forced to write and his hopes rose. Miss Aldersey was an unrelenting antagonist, firmly resolved that this 'living by faith' missionary who disgraced the other Europeans by going about dressed like the Chinese, should never have Maria. Other friends, however, were kinder and more sympathetic, and they arranged for the couple to meet, whereupon Hudson learned that Miss Aldersey was not in fact Maria's guardian. He then wrote to her uncle in London for permission to marry Maria, and Miss Aldersey followed suit—but in a very different vein! All Hudson and Maria could do was wait and pray—letters to England took an interminable time. Two texts which became his mottoes, emerged at this time. He had them written on scrolls and hung on the wall of his sitting room: Ebenezer ('Hitherto hath the Lord helped us') and Jehovah Jireh ('The Lord will provide').

Hudson's faith and experience as a missionary were growing; he had the joy of seeing precious souls responding to the gospel and going on to become workers in the growing church. Every trial only seemed to reveal the hand of God in a new way as he prayed about every situation. For a while he bravely nursed a missionary friend who was dying with smallpox. After the friend's death, Hudson was faced with a new dilemma: he had to burn all the clothes he had been wearing whilst nursing a patient with such a highly contagious and dangerous disease. He had been giving away money he had received to help others more needy than himself—now what was he to wear once he had burned the infected garments? The answer was supplied in a way that Hudson was sure was the hand of God—a box of his belongings which had been lost for over a year, turned up there and then. Something else also arrived at last—the long awaited letter from Maria's guardian uncle in London, and his reply was favourable! They were beside themselves with joy. The only condition was that they had to wait until Maria was twenty-one, which was only a few days away. Her birthday was 16th January 1858, and the wedding day was 20th January!

Two happier people and two people more in love than Hudson and Maria could not be found. They were perfectly matched; Hudson's growing faith inspired Maria, whilst her better education and more refined upbringing enabled her to speedily get rid of some of the rough edges from Hudson's Yorkshire background and make him more genteel in the right way. God was preparing the chosen vessel for greater things and equipping him to mix with the highest levels of society.

The unsettled conditions of that time brought them within a few weeks of their marriage, to settle down to steady missionary work in Bridge Street, Ningpo. They were both kept very busy, Maria teaching in the school, Hudson preaching, teaching and prescribing medicines. God blessed their labours with precious souls who quickly became soul-winners. Their little church was growing and showing much promise.

Within a year of their wedding Maria became pregnant but their early joy was turned to great anxiety when after three months Maria fell desperately ill. In February 1859 it became clear that Maria was dying: her eyes were sunken, her face pinched and pale. Much prayer was made and every remedy tried but in vain. As he waited anxiously by her bedside, another remedy came into Hudson's mind but he felt that he dare not try it without first consulting Dr Parker at the hospital some two miles away. He was afraid to leave Maria

lest she die in his absence, but desperation drove him to feel
he must risk it. On the way he was praying with all his heart
when suddenly the promise of God came powerfully to him:
'Call upon me in the day of trouble: I will deliver thee and
thou shalt glorify Me' (Psalm 50:15). He seized upon it and
pleaded the promise in prayer with quickened faith. Very soon
a deep peace came over him and with it an assurance that his
prayer had been heard. He completed the journey and had his
consultation with Dr Parker who approved the cure Hudson
suggested. However, as soon as Hudson arrived home one
glance told him that Maria was recovering without using any
medicine. God had undertaken. Nearly six months later, on
July 31st, Grace, their first child, was born.

Due to antagonism towards foreigners generated by the
conflict between Britain and China, these were very
dangerous times for Hudson and his wife, but they remained
at their posts whilst many other Europeans left the city. About
a month after the birth of Grace they suffered a great blow
when Dr Parker's wife suddenly died. The doctor then felt
that he should take his four young children back to Scotland,
which would necessitate closing the hospital. He offered the
dispensary to Hudson but there seemed no hope of keeping
the hospital open as Dr Parker had sustained the free beds for
Chinese patients with the fees he charged for treating
Europeans.

Hudson prayed much about his decision and the conviction
deepened as he waited on God for guidance that he should
undertake not only the dispensary but the
hospital—depending on the faithfulness of God to supply the
needs. It was a momentous decision and too much for some of
the hospital staff who resigned when they learned that their
wages could no longer be guaranteed—except by faith!

It was not long before what little money Dr Parker had left
was used up and with it the supplies of food. One morning the
cook informed Hudson that they had just opened the last sack
of rice, which prompted Hudson to reply 'Then the Lord's

time for helping us must be close at hand.' And it was, for a
letter arrived from his faithful friend Mr Berger with a cheque
for £50 and the news that Mr Berger's father had died leaving
him his fortune thus enabling him to send more money to
Hudson. God's provision for the many needs of the hospital
was a testimony to all and convinced many heathens that
Hudson Taylor was serving the Living God. Nine months
later when the toll on his health was such that Hudson had to
take a furlough, the hospital was in better shape financially
than when he took it over. Physically he was exhausted and
felt a trip to England was a necessity if he was to recover. The
Taylor family sailed from China in July 1860 and arrived in
London in November. It was just over seven years since
Hudson had first sailed for China.

Back in England he immediately set about the task of
persuading the Bible Society and the Religious Tract Society
to help in producing a more correct translation of the New
Testament in the Ningpo dialect together with a hymn book,
he also decided to complete his medical studies at the London
Hospital. In all it was to be four years before they would
return to China, but they were busy and important years.
Hudson obtained his medical degree in the late autumn of
1862, after which he concentrated his energies on the revision
of the Ningpo New Testament with Rev F. F. Gough of the
Church Missionary Society. All the time his heart was in
China. A large map of China was on the wall of his study in
their very humble home in Whitechapel, and his burden was
for workers for inland China.

Their homecoming was timely also in that the great 1859
Revival which began in America in 1857 had burst upon
Britain. The churches were full, prayer and evangelism were
the order of the day; new visions and burdens for world
missions also began to grip believers and the Holy Spirit was
at work preparing a new generation of missionaries.
Nevertheless as he travelled around speaking about China
Hudson found that in general people tended to waste time in

responding to a missionary call because they felt they had to wait until God opened the door more emphatically. This he found intolerable when Christ's clear command was 'Go'.

Every week friends gathered with Hudson and Maria in their home in Beaumont Street to pray for China. Their good friend Mr Berger and his wife were regulars, travelling up from their mansion in East Grinstead. The more they prayed the greater became Hudson's burden to make the needs of China known and so he wrote some articles for a Baptist magazine. The editor soon realised that these warranted a wider circulation than his magazine afforded and urged Hudson to write more fully about the claims of Inland China. Busy though he was, he undertook the task, and as he researched for his little book, Hudson discovered that missionaries to China were decreasing. His burden increased to the point of distraction. A million a month were dying without Christ in China.

Throughout the spring of 1865 he prayed and wrestled with God. On Sunday, 25th June ill and tired out, he was spending a few days with the former secretary of the unfortunate Chinese Evangelization Society, George Pearse, in Brighton. Hudson was unable to sit comfortably in a church crowded with a thousand people whilst China's lost millions were dying unevangelised. God had been speaking to him throughout the previous months when other societies had been unwilling to take up the challenge. The whisper became louder: God's voice in his soul said, 'I intend to evangelise Inland China. If you will walk with Me I will do it through you.' He left the church during the singing of the last hymn, wandered out onto the beach and walked alone beside the sea wrestling with his problem. He had learned to trust God for his own needs, and now God was calling him to believe for the needs of others as well. He could hold out no longer; he surrendered himself to God for this great task. He prayed for twenty-four willing, skilful labourers, two for each of the eleven inland provinces which were without a missionary, and two for Mongolia. It was God's responsibility to direct him and provide, Hudson's to obey and follow Him. Peace overflowed his whole being and he recorded his request for twenty-four workers in his Bible. Two days later he opened a bank account in the name of the China Inland Mission with the princely sum of £10. It was the seed-faith which was to produce millions of pounds and hundreds of workers for China.

Hudson completed his first publication and entitled it *China's Spiritual Need and Claims*. It was an immediate success and the secret was that every sentence was steeped in prayer. A second edition was soon called for, and many more editions followed over the years. God opened doors for him and he was given the chance to speak at the Perth Convention (which was equivalent to the Keswick Convention in those days). Firstly Hudson was asked to close one of the great evening meetings in prayer. His simple, fervent prayer lifted the whole meeting so that when he spoke the next day hearts were already open to this quiet young missionary from China. He regaled them with dramatic incidents from his own experience in China and challenged the great congregation with the lost millions in China dying without Christ. Shortly afterwards he was invited to speak at the famous Mildmay Conference in London, and it was here that his book was first distributed. Lord Radstock read it, was deeply impressed and wrote to tell Hudson enclosing a gift of £100 for the work. An invitation to address many of London's high society also followed. Bonds were forged between Hudson and leading Brethren such as Robert Chapman and George Müller, and other prominent Christians, including Lady Beauchamp, William Fry, and Grattan Guinness.

Candidates began to appear in response to Hudson's prayers and public appeals. Money likewise was forthcoming and the dream was at last becoming a reality. During these early years the basic principles of his missionary work were established. The China Inland Mission was to be interdenominational.

The failure of the Chinese Evangelization Society had made him realise that the work must be controlled from the field, not the UK. Further, he was resolved never to appeal for funds and refused to take up offerings in his meetings—he insisted that people send any gifts through the post. All this was revolutionary in those days, but it worked. Hudson wrote his now famous words: 'Depend upon it, God's work done in God's way will never lack God's supplies.'

A meeting in Hertfordshire was chaired by the Dowager Lady Radstock's brother, Colonel Puget; he was so impressed by Hudson's message that he wanted to break the rule and take up an offering, but Hudson refused. The Colonel was rather put out and told him that he himself would have given £5. However, during the night he was so burdened that he could not sleep and came down next morning and handed Hudson a cheque for £500 for China! This enabled Hudson to charter the *Lammermuir* for the forthcoming voyage to China.

Hudson and Maria had four children, Gracie (born in China) and three sons born during the six and a half years they were in England: Herbert, Frederick, and Samuel. Their busy lives and the burden of child-bearing took their toll on Maria's health and she was critically ill for several weeks at the end of 1865. After much prayer it was a tremendous relief to Hudson when his beloved Maria began to recover.

The last day of the year was set apart as a day of prayer and fasting, and it became a regular feature over the years to add fasting to their prayers on special occasions. Hudson's crucial prayer on Brighton beach was answered: he had his twenty-four workers. Six had already sailed for China by the time Hudson prayed that day in Brighton, two more followed, and then Hudson Taylor and Maria and their four children, and sixteen workers (ten women and six men) sailed for China in May, 1866 in the *Lammermuir*. He later wrote: 'The China Inland Mission was born of prayer, nourished by prayer, and sustained only in answer to believing prayer. We rest on God's promises. We do not publish donors' names, we make no collections, we have no reserve funds, we never go into debt; our path now is as much walking on the waters as it was at the beginning'.

The voyage was far from smooth. Hudson's powers of leadership were tested to the full during their months at sea, but his humour, wisdom, patience and prayerful spirit won the day. Firstly the missionaries fell out among themselves, but through prayer and fasting the unity was restored. Several of the crew were converted, but in the South China Sea they were caught in typhoons and storms which battered them mercilessly for fifteen days and almost wrecked the ship. The crew were in a state of mutiny and only Hudson's calm and prayerful intervention saved the day. The Yorkshire lad had come a long way: his leadership was firmly established, which was just as well for from the moment of landing in China they were confronted with opposition and difficulties of every conceivable kind.

The party arrived in Shanghai at the end of September, 1866. Hudson was only too well aware that 'crossing the sea never made a missionary' (a saying he often repeated). However, under his faith-inspiring leadership these raw recruits (with one or two exceptions) were turned into the nucleus of the future great missionary force of the C.I.M.

Hudson's confidence was in God and His Word. He believed 'in the wisdom, as well as the blessedness of literally obeying the Scriptures'. He staked his all on the faithfulness of God and truth of His Word. From the first his plan was the systematic evangelism of the whole of China. His policy was to plant missionaries in the capitals of all the provinces, and then spread out from there. As always he began the new year of 1867 with prayer and it was remarkable that by the end of the year the C.I.M. had thirty-four missionaries in China and had eight stations. Hudson revealed to a friend that the sun had never risen upon China without finding him either praying for or having prayed for, those labouring with him on the field. The morning watch was one of the great secrets of his close walk with God and of his ever-increasing faith. No matter how busy he was, carrying out medical work, burdened with administration, writing scores of letters, or preaching, Hudson always made prayer his priority. Even when travelling he would carry matches and a candle so that waking before dawn to start his quiet time, he could read his Bible by the light of the candle and then pray. Often he prayed lying down, and frequently he woke in the early hours of the morning, had his prayer time and then returned to sleep.

Some five months after their arrival in Hangchow, Maria gave birth to another daughter, Maria Hudson, in February, 1867. Hudson was passionately devoted to his wife and a warm, loving and caring father to his children. It pained him deeply when his frequent journeys separated him from them, sometimes for weeks at a time. When he returned he loved to romp and play with them in the freest and happiest way. He was especially close to Gracie, who had entered into a real experience of salvation on board ship. She was growing into a most affectionate child and the bond between father and daughter was increasingly close. It was therefore a tremendous blow, when shortly after her eighth birthday she was taken ill and died within a matter of days. Hudson had been called away to attend to a lady missionary who was sick, and when he returned Gracie was unconscious. Too late he diagnosed that she was suffering with water on the brain: she died on 23rd August. Hudson and Maria were devastated but they accepted it without bitterness; their deep inner conviction was: 'God makes no mistakes'. The news had a chastening effect on some of the missionaries who were causing trouble and divisions were healed.

Many times their lives and the lives of C.I.M. missionaries were endangered during this period as riots broke out all around them, but their courage and resolve did not fail. Mobs attacked and ransacked their house and they escaped by the skin of their teeth on more than one occasion. When news got out about some of the treatment they and other missionaries and Europeans had received, the British government sent a gunboat up the river as far as Chinkiang. The Chinese apologised and suddenly the hitherto unpopular C.I.M. was being lauded by the European community in Shanghai. In fact Hudson was upset at the show of British force and would much rather have suffered, leaving everything in the hands of God.

When news of the happenings finally trickled through to England, it was at a time of political change; Disraeli's government having given way to Gladstone's, and suddenly the press began to blame the missionaries for causing the trouble in the first place. Some, who should have known better, deliberately stirred up these rumours and before long Hudson Taylor and his 'tin-pot' mission were being blamed in the House of Lords. The Duke of Somerset even urged the recall of British missionaries from China. The adverse publicity and malicious slander caused some loss of support but the main response of Hudson and his many friends was to pray; nevertheless they felt deeply hurt.

Not long after the riots in 1869, Maria gave birth to their fourth son, Charles. The Taylors' courage and Christlike spirit made a great impression on the unconverted and it was their great joy and comfort to welcome more converts during that year. But the pressures told; the fact that China was opening up to the gospel increased their burdens. When the newspapers in Shanghai also attacked Hudson virulently, his already jangled nerves snapped. He was driven to the point of despair and but for the grace of God and the sustaining love of his wife Hudson confessed he would have fainted and broken down.

Hudson was at this stage desperately dissatisfied with his spiritual state and was earnestly seeking the secret of unbroken communion with Christ. Maria was a little mystified at her husband's restlessness because *she* had been enjoying just such an experience for years! Then at last the light dawned upon him, so simply, so sweetly. His missionary colleague, John McCarthy, had been engaged in the same soul quest and wrote to Hudson that God had given him a glimpse at least of what they were seeking: it was a case of abiding rather than striving. For years Hudson had thought abiding was a high attainment to which he was unequal. Suddenly he realised that abiding in Christ was not a struggling effort which requires much strength, but the very opposite—abiding actually required no strength at all. As he read he saw it all; from that moment to the end of his days he knew that abiding in Christ was the secret of everything, and that abiding is not a thing of consciousness, but of fact. 'Do we cease to abide in our homes when asleep at night?' he asked. He saw that our union with Christ 'is a fact, not a feeling. A man is as much one with his wife when asleep as when awake, when abroad as when at home.' The words 'If we believe not, He abideth faithful' took on a new meaning and remained as an anchor to his soul ever after. He was full of it and shared his new understanding with everyone: he was transformed.

However, at the beginning of 1870 China was once again in a dangerous state of agitated unrest which threatened to boil over at any moment. Hudson and Maria decided on the heart-breaking decision to send the four older children home to England (eight year old Bertie, seven year old Freddie, little Samuel who was five and a very delicate child and Maria, three) leaving only the baby, Charles, with them. One of the missionaries, Emily Bletchley, travelled home with them, but poor little Samuel died before they could even leave China and was buried at Chinkiang. It made the parting so much harder for them all. 1870 was a year of the most severe trials for Hudson Taylor, testings which would have crushed and destroyed a lesser man.

The unbearably hot summer of that year witnessed the widespread unrest throughout China boiling over into rebellion, with the foreigners being blamed for the troubles which included the massacre of ten nuns at Tientsin in June, and other such outrages. To make matters worse it seemed that sickness was affecting every one of the C.I.M. stations; Hudson and Maria were kept frantically busy. Although she was in the final stages of pregnancy, Maria insisted on nursing those who were sick. At the beginning of July, Maria went down with cholera; within two days she gave birth to their fifth son, Noel, but she was too weak to nurse him. In less than two weeks baby Noel died, and five days later Maria's beautiful and selfless life came to an end also. Hudson was floored by this double blow. However, like Job, he refused to charge God foolishly and was able to say through his tears, 'The Lord hath given and the Lord hath taken away, blessed be the name of the Lord'. But Hudson's storms were far from over; within a short time he himself went down with ague and dysentery. Separated from his children, bereft of his beloved Maria, his loneliness was suddenly so terrible it could be felt by all, but through it all his new sense of 'abiding in Christ' remained in spite of everything. On the day of prayer and fasting at the close of the year he could write that 'this was the most sorrowful and most blessed year of my life'.

Just over a year later in August 1871, Hudson sailed for England as it was essential for him to come home to make new arrangements for the growing mission and for his family, and it was important also for his health. In November 1871, he married Miss Jennie Faulding, who had been a member of the group which had sailed on the *Lammermuir*.

All the time he was in Britain Hudson was planning and praying for the expansion of the work. By this time they had thirty workers on thirteen stations. God gave him some outstanding British helpers such as George and Henry Solteau, and in August 1872, a Home Council was formed, although the control was still to be with him on the field. Hudson returned to China with his new wife in October 1872, with the vision to claim every city in China for Christ.

Not long after his return to China, during a visit to Western China to establish a centre there, Hudson slipped and fell heavily when coming down the steamer's gangway, resulting in damage to his spine which gradually resulted in paralysis of his legs. By the time he returned home to England in 1874 there was the very real possibility that he would never walk again.

For months Hudson was virtually helpless, having to lie in bed, unable to even write, but one thing he could still do was pray—and this he did 'without ceasing'. Once again the map of China hung on the wall of his room and it is no coincidence that this period of suffering and physical prostration marked the great enlargement of the C.I.M. He prayed and appealed for eighteen more men to enter the still unoccupied provinces. Financially the Mission had been going through a most trying period; more than once they were down to pence not pounds, but nothing could daunt Hudson and the volunteers began to apply. By this time he was beginning to recover sufficiently to be able to sit up in bed for short periods, but there was little rest for he was kept busy interviewing candidates, and the weekly prayer meeting was also held in his room. His burden remained to evangelise the Chinese millions. Hudson recognised that every important advance of the C.I.M. was somehow linked with sickness or suffering, throwing him upon God in special ways. It was a sure sign that they were not wrestling against flesh and blood but against principalities and powers, the spiritual forces of darkness that had dominated China for so long.

In September 1876 Hudson had recovered sufficiently to be able to sail for China for the fourth time. At long last further agreements had been ratified which really opened Inland China in a positive way and Hudson Taylor was resolved to exploit the improved situation to the full. Over the following years the growth of the C.I.M. was spectacular. In December 1877 he was back in England asking for another thirty workers for China. He got his thirty before the end of 1878 and then like Oliver Twist he was soon asking for more. Neither was it just a matter of numbers and getting anybody—the standards he set for his recruits were very high, and although inevitably there were one or two misfits, the majority were excellent missionaries and some were absolutely outstanding.

The C.I.M. and Hudson Taylor began to be internationally recognised at last for their true worth.

In 1883 the appeal went out for seventy new workers; these (and more) were on the field by the end of 1884. In that same year the 'Cambridge Seven' created a great sensation when they announced their decision to go to China and serve with the C.I.M. Some members of the Cambridge Seven were household names including C. T. Studd who played cricket for England. When the 'Seven' sailed for China in 1885 it roused Christians everywhere to the challenge and claims of missionary work.

There was still no stopping or satisfying Hudson Taylor, and in the very next year, 1886, he was praying and appealing for one hundred new workers. By May 1887 the hundred new missionaries had sailed.

Hudson Taylor's name was now known around the world and he received invitations to America, Canada, Scandinavia and Australia, resulting in the spread of the work and more recruits from these lands joining the ever expanding work of the C.I.M. By 1891 the C.I.M. was nearly five hundred strong. In the face of famines and wars, riots and rebellions, sickness and suffering, martyrdoms and deaths, Hudson Taylor pressed onwards, reaching ever further into inland China, praying always and inspiring his colleagues into greater and more daring exploits of faith. However, over the years China was in conflict with Britain, Japan, Russia, France and Germany, and at the close of the century the seething hatred of foreigners finally boiled over in the terrible Boxer riots. It was at this time that the years of strenuous and unsparing service took their toll on Hundson's body and his health finally collapsed. He was forced to leave China in the autumn of 1899.

After spending time in Australia and New Zealand, Hudson travelled on to America and finally arrived in England in June. The Boxer uprising had begun in May and the news of the terrible suffering almost broke his heart. With his wife he went to Switzerland, regretting deeply that he was unable to be in China to share the suffering, but never ceasing to pray. A total of 135 missionaries and fifty-three children were put to death, of whom seventy-nine were connected with the C.I.M. (fifty-eight adults and twenty-one children). At this time the ageing veteran of the Cambridge Seven, D. E. Hoste was appointed as his successor. But Hudson Taylor found this period of enforced inactivity was a great trial: 'It is hardest of all to do *nothing* for His sake,' he said.

After a long and painful illness Hudson's second wife, Jennie, died on July 30th, 1904 and was buried in Switzerland. Her last words to him were 'He will not fail'. A few months after her death he was seized with a great longing to see his beloved China once more and he set sail with his son and daughter-in-law, Dr and Mrs Howard Taylor on February 15th, 1905. He arrived in Shanghai on April 17th, 1905, fifty-one years after his first visit. What a welcome he received during those weeks: everywhere he went he was greeted with reverence.

On Saturday June 3rd he preached to the Chinese Christians in Changsha, and in the afternoon attended a reception with the missionary community in the city. That evening he died, peacefully and suddenly. He was buried most fittingly beside his first wife, Maria, and the children, in Chinkiang.

The secret of Hudson Taylor's life was summed up in three great certainties: 'There is a Living God. He has spoken in the Bible. [Hudson read his Bible through more than forty times]. He means what He says and will do all He has promised.'

He once wrote: 'I have seen God, in answer to prayer, quell the raging of the storm, alter the direction of the wind, and give rain in the midst of prolonged drought. I have seen Him, in answer to prayer, stay the angry passions and murderous intentions of violent men, and bring the machinations of His people's foes to nought. I have seen Him, in answer to prayer, raise the dying from the bed of death, when all human aid was vain; I have seen Him preserve from the pestilence that walketh in darkness, and from the destruction that wasteth at noonday'.

The dominant message of his life, like the recurring theme of a symphony, was the faithfulness of God; 'though we deny Him, yet He abideth faithful, He cannot deny Himself'.

In Hudson Taylor's last official Will and Testament he wrote: 'I trust that in all the days to come, as in the past, we shall recognise our entire dependence upon God and the absolute importance of private and united prayer. How much blessing we owe to our days of prayer, our weekly and daily prayer-meetings, and those of the councils, will never be known on earth'.

Only eternity will reveal how much of the present remarkable survival and growth of the Church in China today stems back to the deep roots implanted through the apostolic labours and prayers of Hudson Taylor, the man who believed God.

3: Charles G. Finney

'Would you like us to pray for you?' said an earnest believer in a Presbyterian prayer meeting to the tall, handsome, young lawyer, who had been attending it for several weeks. 'No', was the blunt reply, 'because so far as I can see, God does not answer your prayers. I suppose I need to be prayed for, but I do not see that it will do any good; you are continually asking but you do not receive. Ever since I came to this town you have been praying for revival but nothing has happened.' Nevertheless, many of them continued to pray for him privately even though their minister, the Rev George Gale, had discouraged them, saying that he did not believe the young man would ever be converted. The minister was in fact a very worried man. Because of the young lawyer's outstanding musical ability he had been put in charge of the choir, but he was such a bad influence upon them that Rev Gale felt that none of the young people would be converted while this sceptical and clever lawyer remained in the town of Adams. 'O Lord, please remove this stumbling-block of a lawyer, Charles Finney, from this town,' was about the only prayer he had any faith to utter. But God had other plans for young Finney who up to that moment in time was completely irreligious.

Charles Grandison Finney was born in Warren, Litchfield County, Connecticut, on August 29th 1792. The Finneys were pioneer stock with English roots, and able to trace their pedigree back to the Pilgrim Fathers. But they were very much the new Americans, proud, independent, and rugged. Charles's father, Sylvester, had fought for American liberty in the War of Independence. That battle won, he married Rebecca Rice and got on with the business of hewing out a living for his growing family on the frontiers of the rapidly expanding new nation. Charles was the seventh child and they slipped in the name of Grandison after the hero in a top novel of the times, *Sir Charles Grandison*, by Samuel Richardson. When Charles was two years old, Sylvester sought new opportunities for his family by moving further west, first to Brotherton for a brief spell, then still not satisfied, he loaded up his ox wagons once more and pushed on through the wilderness beyond the Hudson River to settle at Hanover in Oneida County, New York. At the close of the eighteenth century New York State was still very primitive, frontier country, with few schools and churches. In those conditions it was all too easy for a family to drift spiritually. Sylvester's father had founded a Congregational Church in his community in the days before independence, but somehow in the battle to survive on the frontiers, God was almost forgotten and prayer was squeezed out so that Charles grew up without ever hearing his father pray.

Life was tough in the backwoods but young Charles thrived on it; physically and mentally he had all the makings of a real-life hero. By the time he reached his teens he was outstripping his peers at everything he tackled. He loved the outdoor life; with the demands of felling trees, cutting logs, tilling the virgin soil, and looking after the livestock, he grew strong and tall—he was over six feet and well-proportioned. His father taught him to shoot and he became an expert shot with the long-barrelled flintlock rifle which hung over the door of their farmhouse. He loved to venture out into the surrounding woods where deer, wild pigeons, and turkeys abounded. Hunting was a recreation he continued to enjoy throughout most of his life.

When Charles was fourteen he went to the secondary school at Hamilton and in the two years in which he was there he excelled both in his studies and in sport. The school principal was a good man and he encouraged Charles to study hard to gain a sound classical education and to develop his musical talent. He responded and did well in most subjects but he especially loved music, becoming quite an accomplished performer on the violin and the cello. The latter was his favourite instrument—the full, rich sounds appealed to his manly emotions. In addition he was given singing lessons and encouraged to develop his excellent voice, which had a good range. His love of music remained with him as a priceless asset throughout his life. When it came to sports he swept everything before him—whether it was running, wrestling, or riding, he outstripped all his friends. The restless pioneer spirit was still at work in his father and in 1808 Sylvester uprooted his family yet again in a move to Henderson on the shores of Lake Ontario, near Sackett's Harbour. This gave Charles the opportunity to improve his swimming and to take up rowing and sailing. Henderson was still very much virgin pioneer territory, right out in the wilderness—geographically and spiritually.

At about twenty years of age Charles returned to his native Connecticut, and from there to New Jersey, near New York City where he took up teaching. The position was one where he could continue with his studies as well as teaching. He had an active mind and was keen to learn and took every opportunity that was afforded him to pursue his learning; twice he returned to New England for study periods in high school. As a teacher he was extremely popular; physically and mentally he was head and shoulders above most of his fellows (but spiritually he was still immature). Sport in those days was not so much a matter for pleasure as essential for survival on the frontier; running, riding, shooting, swimming, rowing, jumping, throwing, were all basic skills which pioneer children wanted to acquire—and as Charles could do them all better than most he was their hero, and a good looking one as well.

Charles seriously considered going to Yale University to

further his studies and obtain a degree but his preceptor was a Yale graduate and he persuaded Charles that he could cover the same course by private study in half the time he would have to spend at Yale. It did not work out quite like that, however, but no matter: Charles was popular, proud, self-assured, very personable—and the world was his oyster. A singing school he conducted for a time had been attended by people from miles around. He joined the Freemasons and became a Master Mason in the pursuit of his ambitions to advance his social life. No-one (including himself) had any doubts but that Mr Charles was going places.

Eventually his preceptor invited Charles to join him in a venture to establish an Academy way down in one of the Southern States. The idea appealed to Charles but when he sent word to his parents of the proposal they immediately journeyed over to visit him. They had not seen him for four years and Charles was shocked to see that his mother's health had deteriorated seriously. In the circumstances it did not take much to persuade him that instead of moving south he should return home with them. Back there in Jefferson County, New York State, he contemplated his future and decided that he would like to take up law. Just a few miles away from the Finney home in the town of Adams was the law office of Benjamin Wright, the leading attorney in that part of the state. When the great man offered to take twenty-six year old Charles under his wing for training in law, it seemed that a glittering future lay ahead. The plan was for him to take up law and eventually go into politics. The growing nation needed leaders and Charles had all the qualifications—personality, charm, a keen mind, and the right connections.

The coming of Charles Grandison Finney to take up residence in the small, close-knit community of Adams, caused quite a ripple—especially among the young ladies! Not a few of them found excuses to parade past Mr Benjamin Wright's law office in the hope of catching a glimpse of the handsome young stranger who had just moved in. More than one heart fluttered when news got around that he was an all-round athlete, a teacher, an accomplished musician—and single! Nor was the interest among the fair sex confined to Adams. One young teenager away in Utica found herself praying with great fervency for the young lawyer—what a catch for the cause of Christ if he could be won—not to mention for herself. Young Lydia Andrews had Charles right at the top of her prayer list.

The Presbyterian Church in Adams was very much at the heart of life in the community. Rev George Gale, the minister, was a young man fresh from the famous Princeton University —the centre of the ultra-reformed theology which dominated much of the church life of the new nation—especially Presbyterianism. It was the first chance that Charles really had of being near a church of any standing with a settled, educated ministry. He was not used to keeping Sunday as a special day—in the frontier wilderness one day just ran into the next without any difference. He was enjoying the challenge of law and he took his studies seriously. His keen, logical mind revelled in it and constant contact with an attorney of Mr Wright's ability sharpened up his thinking powers tremendously. Life was full and he much preferred to be out hunting on a Sunday than going to church but eventually he decided that it was the right thing for an up and coming lawyer to do and he started attending church. This raised the pulserates of the church's young ladies and the hopes of the minister. The young Rev George Gale put even more effort and thought into writing out his sermons. Each Sunday he read them out carefully and decorously, word for word, exactly as they were written. That was the Princeton style. He was confident that his academic masterpieces could not fail to impress the young lawyer and he started calling in at the law office to see what effect his sermons were having. Everyone was taken with Finney's charm and the church choir and music had taken a decided turn for the better since his taking it over, but a doubt about Finney's spiritual state niggled at the back of George Gale's mind. His worst fears were soon confirmed, far from being impressed with his brilliant sermon Finney had criticised it unmercifully. The Rev Gale retreated, abashed and somewhat taken aback.

Each Sunday Gale tried harder, working furiously on his sermons, applying all that he had been taught at Princeton, but every Monday his encounters with Finney got worse. The student lawyer was mature and self-assured, and his devastating logic tore Rev Gale and his sermons to pieces; he soon realised to his chagrin that he was no match for Finney in an argument. The man was obviously unregenerate. He could not possibly be one of God's 'elect', but his influence in the town and on the community was growing all the time. The young people he took for music lessons, and the choir, all idolised him. Finney was an excellent dancer but a bad influence on this young group; he was not slow to express his opinions and they usually clashed with those of the minister! Rev Gale began to dread facing those bright blue eyes, which twinkled insolently back at him over the desk in the law office; the man was positively enjoying pulling his beautiful sermons to pieces. Unbelievers were beginning to hide behind Finney's open scepticism.

Rev Gale was only too well aware that the husband of one of the most godly women in his church constantly challenged her with 'If religion is true, why don't you convert Finney?' 'Well, Reverend, what are you going to do about it?' he in turn was asked. What could he do about it?

Then his hopes revived a little when Finney actually started attending the weekly prayer meeting. He had been in the town for three years now and was a junior law partner in the Wright practice. Unknown to Gale or anyone else in Adams, Finney was beginning to search for the truth. In his law studies he constantly found many quotations from the Bible, especially concerning the Mosaic law, and so he went out and purchased a Bible, the first he had ever owned. At first he studied it merely as a textbook along with his other law books and was content for it to lie openly on his desk with the rest of his books. But the living seed began to germinate, exerting its mysterious influence upon his legal mind; the Sword of the Spirit began to wound his awakening conscience. The Bible suddenly became an embarrassment to him. If he was reading it when someone entered the office he would immediately bury it out of sight under his other books. In secret, however, he continued to study it avidly. He was captivated by it and somehow it held him like a magnet.

Although Rev Gale had just about given up on Charles, a number of people were still praying earnestly for his conversion. Several miles away in Utica, pretty, seventeen-year-old Lydia Andrews was just one of a band of praying folk who remembered him constantly in their intercession. She admitted to herself that her prayers were tinged with quite a degree of selfishness; she was hopelessly in love with him, although Charles was completely unaware of her existence. She was twelve years younger and little more than a child when she had first seen him: too young for Charles to notice then—but later he did with a vengeance.

Finney was now twenty-nine years of age and as he read his Bible his trained legal mind grasped two great essentials. If the Bible is true—all men are lost sinners and ought to be told in the clearest way their condition and the way of salvation. If the Bible is trustworthy, those who pray ought to believe God and obtain definite answers to their prayers. Both seemed the very opposite of what he found in the church at Adams. Rev Gale's sermons seemed to him to be full of contradictions; the man told people to repent and then proceeded to tell them they could not repent, that being a matter entirely for God! The prayers at the prayer meeting droned on week after week without ever seeing—or expecting—an answer. It was all so confusing and exasperating but the Bible itself seemed so very clear.

Nevertheless the Spirit of God was at work not only in Finney's heart but in the surrounding area as well. One day when he was returning from a legal appointment Finney overheard a man praying in a schoolhouse—it was praying of a different kind to any that he had ever heard in the weekly prayer meeting, and he admitted that it made a bigger impact upon him than anything he had heard up to that point. Things were coming to a head and on the second Sunday of October 1821, he determined that he would settle the question of salvation as soon as possible. With that in mind he arranged to keep himself free on Monday and Tuesday so that he could give himself to reading the Bible and praying. By Tuesday night Charles was deeply convicted of his need; for a time he felt as if he was going to die and he knew that if he did he would be lost. Early next morning, after an uneasy night, Finney was again reading his Bible, before leaving his place of lodging to walk to the office. Just as he arrived there an inward voice seemed to ask him: 'What are you waiting for? Did you not promise to give your heart to God? What are you trying to do? Are you endeavouring to work out a righteousness of your own?' At that very moment the whole plan of God's salvation in Christ seemed to open itself to him in the clearest possible way. He saw very definitely the reality and fullness of the atonement of Christ, and that His work on the cross was a finished work—full and complete. He understood that all that was necessary on his part was to give his own consent to yield up his sins and accept the Saviour. There he stood on the street with these thoughts flashing through his mind, then came the question to his heart, 'Will you accept it today?' He determined there and then that he would accept it that very day or die in the attempt.

Instead of going into his office Charles turned around and made for a secluded spot in the woods over the hill, feeling that he must be alone to pray without interruption. But on this misty autumn morning he found himself so afraid of being seen going into the woods to pray that he skulked along the fence until he was completely out of sight of the town. Even in the seclusion of the trees he found himself alarmed at every rustle among the leaves—ashamed in case anyone find him on his knees. When it dawned upon him that this sensation was nothing but pride, he was overwhelmed with remorse and cried out at the top of his voice that he would not leave that place if all the world could see him. Immediately the Scripture flashed into his mind 'You shall seek me and find me, when you shall search for me with all your heart'. Finney laid hold of that promise and immediately other passages from the Bible came flooding into his mind, bringing peace and comfort. He left the woods to find that he had passed the whole morning there, although it seemed to him that he had been there only a short time.

After spending the afternoon in his office Charles determined that when everyone had left for the day he would spend the evening alone in prayer. No sooner had he seen the senior partner, Mr Wright, to the door, than he felt an overwhelming desire to pray. He rushed into the back office where there was neither fire nor light, yet it seemed to him as though the room was full of light. As he shut the door Christ appeared to him. Charles later said, 'It seemed as if I met the Lord Jesus Christ face to face. It did not occur to me then, nor did it for some time afterward, that it was wholly a mental state. On the contrary, it seemed to me that I saw Him as I would see any other man. He said nothing, but looked at me in such a manner as to break me right down at His feet. I have always since regarded this as a most remarkable state of mind, for it seemed to me a reality that He stood before me, and I fell down at His feet and poured out my soul to Him. I wept aloud like a child, and made such confessions as I could with my choked utterance.'

After this wonderful experience Finney returned to the front office and was just about to sit down when suddenly he received a mighty baptism of the Holy Ghost. He described it graphically; 'Without any expectation of it, without ever having thought in my mind that there was any such thing for me, without any recollection that I had ever heard the thing mentioned by any person in the world, the Holy Spirit descended upon me in a manner that seemed to go through me body and soul. I could feel the impression, like a wave of power, going through and through me. Indeed, it seemed to come in waves and waves of liquid love, for I could not express it in any other way. And yet it did not seem like water but rather the breath of God. I can recollect distinctly that it seemed to fan me, like immense wings; and it seemed to me as these waves passed over me, that they literally moved my hair like a passing breeze.

'No words can express the wonderful love that was shed abroad in my heart. I wept aloud with joy and love; and I do not know but I should say I literally bellowed out the unutterable gushings of my heart. These waves came over and over and over me, one after another, until I recollect I cried out, "I shall die if these waves continue to pass over me". I said, "Lord, I cannot bear any more", yet I had no fear of death.'

Eventually he went home to bed but next morning when he awakened with the sunlight streaming into his room, the baptism he had received the previous night returned upon him in the same manner. He knelt up in bed and wept aloud with joy; it was impossible for him to doubt any more: he was truly converted; he was a child of God.

At last Finney regained his composure and made his way to the office. When Mr Benjamin Wright, the Attorney, arrived he told him of his experience and spoke a few words to him about salvation. The effect was instantaneous and remarkable. Mr Wright stared at his junior partner in astonishment. He stood there for a few moments absolutely dumbstruck then left the office. Finney later discovered that his remarks had pierced him like a sword and he did not recover from it until he was converted.

Soon afterwards a client entered and said: 'Do you recollect that my case is to be tried at 10.00 am this morning?' The man was a deacon in the church and he was amazed when Finney replied, 'I have a retainer from the Lord Jesus Christ to plead His cause and I cannot plead yours.' Finney went on to explain something of what had happened and told him he would have to find someone else to attend to his law-suit, he could no longer do it; Christ had enlisted him for His cause.

Finney had an overwhelming conviction that God had called him to preach the gospel and that he had to begin immediately. Thereupon he left the office determined to witness to every person he met about Christ. It seemed that everyone he spoke to on that memorable day was brought under deep conviction resulting subsequently in their salvation.

The news of Finney's conversion spread like wildfire through the town of Adams. Knowing the Finney of old, more than one (including the Rev Gale) said they did not believe it, and an old lawyer in the town actually said it was all a hoax perpetrated by Finney on Christians. That night, without any prior arrangement people flocked to the church until it was packed to capacity. Finney stood up and told what had happened to him; most were deeply impressed, but one or two left saying that there was no mistaking his earnestness, but he was obviously deranged. Nightly meetings followed for a long time and many were converted. The young people on whom he had had such an influence were all converted with just one exception. Unconsciously Charles had begun his career as a revivalist.

The work spread among all classes and out to the surrounding villages. He visited his parents at Henderson: they both found Christ and the work of grace spread there also. In the first week after his conversion Finney had no desire to eat or sleep, but wisely after that he took better care of himself, realising that his health was a precious gift of God.

Several of the local people went out to the same spot in the woods where Finney had been converted and returned to testify that they had found peace with God. Finney's boss, Benjamin Wright, Attorney, heard these testimonies, but felt that such a thing was beneath his dignity; he was perfectly able and willing to pray in his own sitting room. Somehow, though, he did not seem to be getting anywhere. He even spent a whole night in prayer but the morning found him more distressed than ever. Then one afternoon when Finney was sitting in his office a young man burst in exclaiming, 'Attorney Wright is converted'. He told how he had gone into the woods to pray and had heard someone in the valley shouting very loudly. When he went to investigate he found Mr Wright walking to and fro, and singing at the top of his voice. Every few moments he would stop and clap his hands together vigorously and shout at the top of his voice, 'I will rejoice in the God of my salvation.' Looking out of the window as the young man was telling all this, Finney saw Mr Wright coming into view at the bottom of the hill, where he witnessed his boss meeting up with an old Methodist. Mr Wright embraced this old man warmly and lifted him off his feet. By the time he arrived in the office he was sweating profusely, all his dignity gone, and he was shouting 'I've got it! I've got it!' He confessed to them all that he realised it was his pride which had been hindering him. From that moment the well known Attorney took a definite stand for God.

In the year following Finney's conversion some sixty-three people were added to the local Presbyterian Church. It was a time of revival blessing but even so, by the spring of the following year (1822) the zeal of many was beginning to cool a little and the prayer meetings were not so well attended. Charles had already established the habit of rising early in the morning to pray, and soon he persuaded others to join him. When they started to cool off he would call round at their houses to encourage them. One morning when he had gone round a number of houses doing this, he arrived at the meeting-house to find that only Rev Gale was there. It was dawn and suddenly it seemed to Finney that the glory of God shone all around him in the most marvellous way; so great was the manifestation that he was almost prostrated on the ground. In this light it seemed to him that he could see all nature praising God—except man—and the revelation overwhelmed him. He felt he understood at that moment something of the light that had prostrated Paul on the Damascus road. It was a light he knew he could not endure for long. He burst out into loud weeping to the astonishment of Rev Gale who apparently saw nothing. When he had finished weeping and the vision was over he was left with his mind in great calm. Finney had quite a number of similar remarkable experiences over the years which followed, but they were so vivid and precious that he shrank from saying much about them, except on rare occasions to people he felt could appreciate such happenings.

After some months Charles Finney was accepted as a candidate for the Presbyterian ministry, and he placed himself under the local presbytery to prepare himself. The presbytery wanted him to enrol at Princeton Theological Seminary, which to most of them represented the pinnacle of Christian learning, the great citadel of ultra-reformed Calvinistic Theology. Finney staggered them, especially Princeton-trained Rev Gale, by stubbornly refusing to go. When pressed he bluntly told them that his reason for not going was that he considered Princeton did not provide the proper training to make men effective ministers of the gospel. They were aghast at his audacity but agreed to place him instead under the superintendency of Rev Gale for training and study.

This arrangement turned out to be a farce. His sessions with Rev Gale turned into endless bouts of bitter controversy and fierce debate. Finney could not stomach the extreme hyper-Calvinism which Rev Gale propounded and said so in no uncertain terms. The various confessions of the church weighed more with Mr Gale than the Bible, but Finney was persuaded that the Bible was the inspired Word of God and he sought to test everything by that and that alone. At one stage Charles was so discouraged with this endless controversy that he was on the point of giving up studying for the ministry altogether. Fortunately for him there was a very godly, praying elder in the church who encouraged him, especially in prayer, and he came through the trial more determined than ever to preach the truth as he saw it in the Bible. Rev Gale confessed that he had never won a single soul to Christ that he knew of, yet he insisted that if Finney was to succeed he must do it all the Princeton way; he must write out his sermons word for word, and then read them in the pulpit. Finney found this method impossible; he preferred to steep himself in the Word of God, spend much time in prayer, and then depend upon God inspiring him. For him extempore preaching was the only way.

After some months the Presbytery met to examine Charles and hear him preach with a view to deciding whether he should be granted a licence to preach the gospel in Presbyterian churches. At Rev Gale's insistence he had duly written out his sermon for the occasion, but once he began to preach he could not contain himself and he departed from the script and preached extemporaneously. Nevertheless the Presbytery voted unanimously in favour of his being licensed.

Not having had regular training for the ministry he did not expect to preach in the cities but was content to start in the new settlements. His first efforts were in two villages some sixteen miles apart; Evans' Mills and Antwerp. The results were typical of Finney's life-work. His aims were twofold: to arouse the church (especially nominal Christians) and to awaken the unsaved and bring them to a definite commitment to Christ. He presented his case with the ruthless logic of a lawyer, but it was logic on fire from lips that had been touched with a live coal from God's altar. At Evans' Mills the people at first were so incensed against Finney that they decided to tar and feather him. But after Finney and a deacon spent a day in prayer and fasting, the Spirit of God came so mightily upon Finney as he preached that it was like opening a battery of cannons on the congregation. In the following days there were many conversions. The scenes witnessed under Jonathan

Edwards, George Whitefield, and John Wesley were repeated; sinners were gripped with awesome conviction, strong men swooned and groaned. But he did not leave them there: he preached the whole counsel of God; he preached the Word of God; he presented Christ. Often for one, two, even three hours he would unfold gospel truths, grappling with errors of the day in which many had taken refuge, such as universalism (that there is no such thing as endless punishment and in the end all men will be saved), and unitarianism (which denied not only the Trinity but nearly all the great gospel truths). After arousing the conscience, then by tearful tenderness he would persuade the heart and move the will to choose Christ and openly declare it.

After preaching in one meeting at Evans' Mills, one prominent lady in the church was so overcome with conviction that at first it seemed that she had fainted. When Finney saw her he realised what had happened and told her friends to take her home. There she lay speechless for some sixteen hours; then when she 'came to' she did so with great rejoicing. She publicly acknowledged that for years she had been deceived into thinking that she was a Christian, but as Finney had preached she had a view of the holiness of God which made her realise her need of Christ. Her testimony had a great effect on many others in the church who were trusting in their own righteousness and good works.

On another day in that same place, Finney was asked by one man to visit his dying sister, whose husband was a strong universalist. The man took Finney to see her when the husband was out, knowing that the man was bitterly opposed to his preaching. Finney led the dying woman to Christ and she died peacefully showing every evidence of a real work of grace in her heart. When her husband found out what had happened he was so incensed that he armed himself with a pistol and went to the meeting vowing that he would kill Finney. The building was packed and Finney was oblivious of his would-be assassin. As he preached, suddenly this powerfully built man fell from his seat, groaning with conviction and crying out that he was slipping into hell. The people all knew him although he was a stranger to Finney. The man had to be helped home but early next morning he went out into the woods and after a time of earnest prayer he too found Christ as his Saviour. He came into town and when he saw Finney on the street he was so full of joy at what had happened that he picked Finney up in his arms and swirled him round two or three times, and then told him of his conversion. The effect upon the little community of around one and a half thousand people was dramatic.

Another convert was the foul-mouthed, blaspheming, owner of a low tavern in the town. He cursed all the Christians he met but after special prayer was made for him by the believers, this man also came to a meeting intending to make a disturbance but soon came under such conviction that he writhed in his seat. He publicly confessed his sins and turned to Christ. He went back and cleaned up his tavern and started a prayer meeting every night. It was a revival—a visitation of God.

Finney was doing this work as a missioner under the auspices of a women's missionary society and it was while he was there receiving his commissioning from them that his eyes first alighted upon the young lady who had been praying for him (with mixed motives) for so long. She was in the meeting at a place called Utica where she just happened (!) to be visiting an aunt. Although he saw her only very briefly on this occasion, Charles was immediately smitten and could not get this beautiful young lady out of his mind. Even during his prayers he found that his mind was turning to the attractive Miss Lydia Root Andrews. She was only twenty years of age and he was thirty-two but it was a love-match. As soon as Charles proposed (and it was not long delayed) she accepted, disclosing to him that she had loved him secretly ever since she was a small girl and had prayed with others for many years for his salvation.

Their lightning romance was sealed in marriage in October 1824 but needless to say Lydia's love and dedication were immediately put to the test. After the briefest of honeymoons, Charles rode back to Evans' Mills to arrange for their move there to set up their new home, planning to return for his bride a few days later. Just before leaving Evans' Mills for the wedding he had preached at a village called Perch River. As soon as they heard that Charles was back from honeymoon they sent an urgent message to him to come and preach as revival was breaking out as a result of his first visit! He went and ministered, intending to travel back for Lydia the next day, but the Spirit of God began to move with such power among them that he felt he dared not leave. The move of God spread to another village called Brownsville with a population of nearly two thousand and such was the situation when Charles visited them that again he felt compelled to stay on. He sent a message to his new wife explaining the delay; then winter set in and travel became virtually impossible until next spring. It was a difficult winter for both of them: Charles found that he had a tremendous spiritual battle on his hands at Brownsville and dear Lydia bowed graciously to this trial of her love and faith and declared she would wait until God opened the door for them to be reunited. She was a rare person, a God-given treasure of a wife to Charles. They enjoyed twenty-three very happy years together; their marriage was blessed with six children, two of whom died in childhood but the remaining four all distinguished themselves.

The early days of Charles' ministry in the area around Evans' Mills were tremendous days in which God's power was demonstrated in revival power and which laid the foundation for his future service. The village of Antwerp was just a few miles north of Evans' Mills; Finney arrived there to find that the services in the brick-built Meeting House had been discountinued for some time and it was kept locked up. He arranged for a meeting in the local school and very soon the people were thronging to hear him, with many being converted. On his third Sunday there an old man from a neighbouring village some three miles down the road asked him to preach there as they never had any services. Finney consented and went on Monday, having agreed with the old man he would come if the old man would make all the necessary arrangements to announce the meeting. Finney arrived and gave out a hymn, but the singing was so awful—they bawled very loudly and so out of tune—that Finney with his trained musical ear literally put his hands over his ears and got down on his knees and prayed until they had finished. The Spirit of God came upon him as he did so and the Lord gave him a text—he had deliberately not chosen his subject, feeling he should wait until he had assessed the congregation. He was not even sure just where the text was to be found which he felt impressed upon his heart, but he stood up and delivered it: 'Up, get you out of this place; for the Lord will destroy this city.' He knew that it came from the story of Abraham and Lot and the city of Sodom and so he expounded the story in his own way. The more he spoke the more he could see the people looking angry; he then applied the Word to them in a particular and pointed way—throughout his life Finney was never one to play with words. (Even his wife Lydia once said to him that although she knew he loved her, yet she was quite terrified when the power of God came upon him as he preached—standing there like a mighty angel wielding the flashing sword of judgment.) As he pressed home the truth of God upon this rough crowd of backwoods people they suddenly began to fall from their seats all over the building, crying out for God to have mercy on them. Finney said he could not have cut them down quicker if he had literally had a sword in his hand. Within two minutes they were all either prostrated on the floor or on their knees praying loudly. The old man who had invited Finney sat there in the midst of it all looking around him in bewildered amazement, until Finney shouted to him above the noise of weeping and crying to pray. This the old man did immediately in a very loud voice but no one took any notice of him—all were under such deep conviction and concerned only about their own lost souls. Finney knew that the Spirit of God was mightily at work among them and rejoiced. He began to deal with some of them individually and as he pointed them to Christ, one after another found peace with God. It was time then for him to leave for another appointment and he left them in charge of the old man. When he returned next day he discovered that the meeting had continued all night, with many of them still there, and they had finally to be carried away to make way for the school. Finney then found out the reason for the angry reaction to his text: the place was known as Sodom and the only good man in the place was the old man who had invited him and whom they nicknamed Lot! They thought that Finney had deliberately chosen his text because of this, but he was completely ignorant of it all and preached without any inhibitions because he knew God had given him the text as he prayed. The work was lasting and many years later Finney met one young man who had been converted on that memorable day and had subsequently been called to the ministry.

For the first twelve years of his ministry Finney never wrote a word of his sermons. He saturated himself with the Word of God and in prayer, and often went into the pulpit not knowing what he was going to preach on, but again and again the Holy Spirit prompted a particular text or passage to him and when he began to speak he was so inspired that he even surprised himself at the way the Spirit of God opened the Scriptures as he preached. Prayer was the great secret of his life; Finney gave himself continually to prayer in the most intense way. If ever he found the anointing of the Spirit lifting from his life he would spend a day praying (usually with fasting) and the anointing would be renewed.

Finney's preaching was refreshingly different to the boring, written, intellectual essays, which were read by so many ministers of his day—and went right over the heads of most of the hearers. He was accused of being colloquial, of 'letting down the dignity of the pulpit', and of preaching in everyday language. Before his conversion, as a lawyer he used ornate language, but as a minister he deliberately sought to preach so that his hearers understood every word. He used stories and illustrations which matched his hearers—and they listened. Frequently he preached for two hours but people were gripped. He addressed them as a lawyer would a jury seeking a verdict, and more often than not he gained the verdict he was seeking—surrender to the Christ of God.

Finney was once asked at a moment's notice to preach to the Presbytery, and when he did so he chose to stay out of the pulpit which was very high and preached walking up and down the aisle. This offended some of the ministers but his preaching was with such power that it was hard to deny that God was with him. He was ordained on July 1st 1824 as a full Presbyterian minister, some six months after being licensed to preach.

Early in Finney's ministry he met with Rev Daniel Nash who was to become a vital factor in his life. Nash had been spiritually cold for a time until an eye complaint confined him to a darkened room for many hours each day. In his enforced seclusion, unable to read he began to pray and the Spirit of God taught him the secrets of intercession. He emerged from this experience renewed and a mighty intercessor. Many times he would join Finney in the places where he was labouring; they prayed together for many hours, and frequently Nash would give himself to prayer as Finney preached. It was a successful partnership which again and again saw great breakthroughs in the darkest and toughest areas. 'Father' Nash (as he became known) was not popular with everyone—he prayed long and loudly! Even when he retired to the woods his voice could be heard over a great distance. A bitter opponent in one town heard Nash praying in the woods as he was travelling through; although he could not hear what

Nash was actually saying, he was seized with conviction and had no peace until he surrendered to Christ. Finney and Nash stormed heaven together for the souls of men and women, and God heard and answered in such power that thousands upon thousands were swept into the Kingdom of God.

Finney was not the only person God was using in those days, but he became one of the greatest and best known of them all. Revival came to many areas during Finney's years of ministry; there were several visitations of God which influenced wide areas, culminating in the nationwide visitation of 1857.

Over the years Finney rose to increasing prominence. During the first nine years of his ministry he itinerated an ever-growing area; this was between 1824 and 1832. The revival at a place called Western, (a small town, well situated on the eastern shore Oneida Lake, in New York State) and which spread throughout the whole area, brought his name to the fore. Rev Gale had settled in that area for his health; when the two of them met up again they resumed their old verbal duels, but eventually Rev Gale admitted that he realised he was wrong in many things, and even questioned whether he had ever been truly born again. He surrendered his life afresh to Christ and became a firm supporter of Finney thereafter.

Conversions were not limited to any one class; his ministry was especially used of God to the conversion of a considerable number of lawyers and judges, as well as doctors and businessmen. In fact, he stated that he found it easier to preach to lawyers than any other class. There were constant manifestations of what can only be termed supernatural demonstrations of God's power. One Sunday in a place called Rome three men had spent the day drinking and ridiculing the revival. They continued all day until suddenly one of them dropped down dead. People were awed, feeling certain that it was a divine judgment. In twenty days some five hundred solid conversions took place. In the neighbouring town of Utica, a sceptical bank president was convicted and came forward to openly confess Christ as Saviour and Lord. The presence of God overshadowed whole towns during such times. The sheriff of the county was another mocker; he was based in Utica and joked a lot about the revival in nearby Rome. But one day when he had to visit Rome on duty, driving his one-horse sledge, as soon as he crossed the town boundary he was overcome with conviction which he could not shake off but rather increased as he moved further into the town. He had a job to stop himself from weeping and within a few weeks he too was converted.

Finney was no fanatic; the means he used were basically the same throughout his long ministry: preaching, prayer—privately and collectively—and personal dealing with people who were awakened to their spiritual need. He opposed 'wild fire' preaching and never encouraged screaming or outlandish behaviour, although he was never afraid to let the Holy Spirit work in His own way. He introduced the so-called 'anxious seat' at one stage in his ministry; this aroused some opposition but it was a very mild measure. It was simply a matter of inviting those who were concerned about their salvation to come forward to occupy seats at the front in order that they may be dealt with more personally.

More than once God met with Finney in remarkable ways, and from such encounters he always emerged renewed and more greatly empowered. One such occasion occurred in 1826 during the revival at a place called Auburn. As he was praying one day the Lord gave him a vision of what lay before him. The experience was so real that Finney literally trembled and shook from head to foot under the sense of God's Almighty presence. He was humbled before God and then followed a great lifting up when God assured him that He would be with him and that no opposition would prevail against him. Such assurances were needed in the face of some of the bitter and violent opposition which he had to encounter to the end of his days.

Around the 1830s a revival in the Columbia region paved

the way for Charles to come to New York City. The Unitarians always criticised him unmercifully, calling him 'a half-crazed fanatic'. A Unitarian businessman of considerable wealth, Lewis Tappan of Boston, was visiting his brother Arthur in New York City, and Lewis said that Finney claimed to be 'the brigadier-general of Jesus Christ'. Arthur denied this, whereupon Lewis wanted to bet his brother five hundred dollars that he could prove it was true. Arthur was an earnest and orthodox Christian who refused to bet but said he would give him five hundred dollars to spend investigating and proving whether the claim was true or false once and for all. Lewis investigated the matter thoroughly and was ultimately convinced that the statements put out by the Unitarians about Finney were utterly false; as a result he left Unitarianism and soon became a born-again believer and an ardent supporter of Finney. In 1832 Lewis Tappan along with some other Christian businessmen, leased an old New York City theatre on Chatham Street, renovated it for a church and invited Finney to pastor it. This he did joyfully, but soon after he was installed, cholera broke out in the city and Finney went down with the dreaded plague; he was unable to preach for a considerable time but eventually he recovered. When he resumed preaching, he quickly adjusted to the special situation in New York. Soon hundreds of conversions occurred, and another church was planted as the work grew. Before he left they had planted seven Free Presbyterian churches in the city.

Disagreements with the Presbyterians eventually resulted in Finney leaving Presbyterianism for Congregationalism. Some of his supporters got together to erect the famous Broadway Tabernacle, a Congregational Church, and Finney became the pastor. But in 1834 his health was suffering so much that he was compelled to take a long sea voyage in an attempt to recover his strength. He went to the Mediterranean but unfortunately he chose the wrong time of year and the Mediterranean proved to be very stormy! He was away for about six months and returned not much improved, but on the homeward voyage he became concerned in case the revival spirit should decline, and a spirit of prayer came upon him. He spent a day in his cabin seeking the face of God in an agony of intercession wrestling with an intensity that was unique even for him. Finally he prevailed and was given an assurance that the work would go forward and that God still had a work for him to do. On his return to New York he found that the young editor of a Christian paper he had founded had been unwise in some areas, resulting in the circulation falling rapidly. He asked Finney if he could write a series on revivals to boost the circulation again; Finney agreed to pray about the matter and then felt he should comply. He delivered his lectures and the editor reported them more or less verbatim, (although the editor had no shorthand and much of it had to be reconstituted from his longhand notes). The series was an immediate success and subsequently they were also published in book form. They sold as fast as they could be printed and were published with equally great success in Britain and in Europe (in French). Finney was sure that the tremendous effect his lectures had worldwide, with many reporting revivals as a result of reading them and putting them into practise, was the consequence of that never-to-be-forgotten day of prayer on the ship. William Booth acknowledged his debt to these lectures.

In the summer of 1835 Finney agreed to divide his ministry more or less equally between the Broadway Church in New York (in winter) and a new Theological College at Oberlin in the summer. He did this for some three years but the burden proved too much and he resigned from the New York pastorate and moved permanently to Oberlin. There, in addition to the College, he also pastored the First Congregational Church in Oberlin.

Finney's work at the College was outstandingly successful in training a whole army of young men for the ministry; they were men of faith and prayer, stimulated by the example as well as the teaching of Finney.

In 1847 Finney was heart-broken when his beloved wife Lydia died, but out of this sad experience he entered into a new experience of holiness, from which sprang his teaching on sanctification. Here again this became a subject of controversy but many were helped into a closer walk with God as a result.

Finney visited the United Kingdom twice, and both occasions were greatly blessed, resulting in the salvation of many and the inspiring of great numbers of Christians to give themselves to prayer for revival. His first visit was in 1849, with his second wife, Elizabeth, a widow, whom he had married in 1848. He preached in a number of towns and cities, including three months in Birmingham (which was the home of Unitarianism—a fact he took great delight in hitting out against!) He also preached with considerable success in London. A wealthy man in Worcester offered to build Finney a mobile tabernacle capable of seating over four thousand. But Finney turned down the offer and lived to regret it, finding that the church buildings in Britain were mostly too small for his purpose, as well as being poorly ventilated. He also found the denominational differences stronger than in America and felt this also was a hindrance to revival.

Finney's second visit took place in 1858, at the time when the Great Revival was just breaking out. During that visit there was a great move of God at Bolton among the Methodists. Some of them became so enthusiastic that he had to restrain them! When sinners began to respond the Methodists of Bolton began to pound the benches and prayed so loudly that the converts were distracted. Finney eventually succeeded in changing this and although there was less excitement there were more converts.

Finney continued as President of Oberlin College until 1866, and under his prayerful leadership it became one of the greatest and best attended colleges of the day. Although he always majored on evangelism, he was not afraid to express himself boldly and eloquently on the great issues of his times.

He was unrelenting in his opposition to slavery and boldly and fearlessly embraced the cause of Abolition. He was equally opposed to the use of alcohol and was vehement in his advocacy of temperance. Although a Freemason before his conversion he soon severed his links with it and opposed it most emphatically. Finney's influence inspired by the gospel had great social consequences for good. Many of his converts were successful businessmen and under his teaching many of them furthered needed reforms in society and with their generous philanthropy relieved poverty.

Finney retired from Oberlin in 1872 but still had three more years of student involvement. To the end of his days he remained a handsome, erect figure of a man, kneeling only to God and the cause of Christ in revival and evangelism. To the end of his days his zeal remained unabated. He lectured and preached shortly before his death which came peacefully on August the 16th, 1875, just a few days short of his eighty-third birthday. On his pulpit were inscribed the words: 'From this pulpit for many years Charles G. Finney presented to this community and to the world the unsearchable riches of Christ'.

Over a hundred years after his death men and women all over the world are still revelling in some of the riches Finney left to the world in his lectures on revival and his teaching on prayer. Many who are engaged in spiritual warfare are finding that Finney still has much to teach us of that heavenly art. He once wrote: 'Truth, by itself, will never produce the effect, without the Spirit of God, and the Spirit is given in answer to prayer. Probably in the Day of Judgment it will be found that nothing is ever done by the truth, used ever so zealously, unless there is a spirit of prayer somewhere in connection with the presentation of truth. But to expect the conversion of sinners by prayer alone, without the employment of truth, is to tempt God'.

4: David Brainerd

When news reached a notoriously ferocious tribe of Red Indians at the Forks of Delaware that a very pale 'paleface' was travelling alone in their direction, a group of them immediately set out to find him and kill him. Tracking their way swiftly and silently through the deep forests they knew so well, it was not long before they located him. The white stranger had erected his tent and was inside it. They crept up on him as soundless as shadows, their dark cruel eyes fixed mercilessly on their prospective victim who was oblivious of their presence. The tall paleface was kneeling in prayer but an even deadlier enemy had beaten them to it. They watched with mixed feelings and bated breath as a rattlesnake slithered right up to the praying figure. It reared its vicious head and flicked out its forked tongue almost in his face—they waited for it to strike. Instead, to their amazement and for no apparent reason, it recoiled and retreated swiftly away through the brushwood.

The Indians shook their heads in disbelief and retired just as silently and swiftly. Out of earshot they exclaimed in wonderment, 'The Great Spirit is with this paleface.'

Unaware of the deadly enemies who had come within such close proximity of him, David Brainerd continued praying, conscious only of being in the presence of Almighty God with a burden for the souls of the savage Indians whose nearby settlement he planned to visit the next day.

He had been warned of the dangers he faced in attempting to communicate Christ to these fierce people, but such was the burning passion in his heart to win them that he was prepared to die in the attempt if need be. To his astonishment, however, when he rode into their settlement the next day just after dawn, the whole tribe came out of their wigwams and welcomed him with reverence and awe. Neither were they wrong in their assessment of this very special servant of God.

The name of David Brainerd is still a name to conjure with, for nearly 250 years the record of his life and labours among the Indians of North America has inspired countless lives. John Wesley speaking at one of the early Methodist Conferences in England said, 'What can be done to revive the work of God where it has decayed?' He answered his own question by declaring: 'Let every preacher read carefully *The Life of David Brainerd.*' The father of modern missions, Baptist, William Carey, followed Wesley's advice and through reading Brainerd's *Life* he was inspired to attempt great things for God in India. Brainerd's biography made Henry Martyn into a missionary, while the great twentieth century missionary statesman and evangelist, Oswald J. Smith writes: 'So greatly was I influenced by the life of David Brainerd in the early years of my ministry that I named my youngest son after him. Brainerd it was who taught me to fast and pray I learned that greater things could be wrought by daily contact with God than by preaching.

When I feel myself growing cold I turn to Brainerd and he always warms my heart. No man ever had a greater passion for souls.'

David Brainerd was blessed with a godly pedigree. His great grandfather, Rev Peter Hobart, had left the shores of England because of persecution and sailed for America in search of religious liberty. One of his five sons, Jeremiah, became a preacher like his father and his last pastorate was in Haddam, Connecticut. Jeremiah's daughter married Hezekiah Brainerd and David was born on April 20th, 1718 in Haddam. He had four brothers and four sisters, but tragedy visited this happy little family: first the father died, when David was only nine, and five years later he lost his mother. Small wonder that he grew up a sad and serious boy with an inclination to depression.

His mother's death especially affected him, caused when a wave of severe sickness swept through the little town. David took to reading his Bible and he hoped he was converted but confessed that he did not really understand what conversion was. He prayed much but the truth about salvation by faith and the new birth eluded him. His struggles continued throughout his teen years, fluctuating from deep concern and being very religious and becoming self-righteous, to melancholy and despair as he unsuccessfully sought salvation by works and religious duties.

A year after his mother's death David moved to East Haddam where he spent four years before going to work on a farm at Durham, when he was nineteen. He was blessed with a very keen intellect and he desperately wanted to improve his education by further study. Although he was still not truly converted he began to feel a strong desire to leave farming and train for the ministry.

In April, 1738, when he was twenty years of age, David went to live with the Rev Fiske in Haddam, who advised him not to associate with young people but to spend his time with older people who were serious and grave, and as a result of this advice he became even more self-righteous and religious in a pious outward sense but not where it really mattered, in the heart. After the death of Rev Fiske he continued his studies with his own brother.

The crisis finally occurred during the winter of 1738 and 1739. In February David set apart a day for fasting and prayer and spent most of the time crying to God for mercy and asking Him to open his eyes concerning sin and the way of life in Christ. Those prayers were heard and the Spirit of God began to reveal to him his sinfulness and the uselessness of all his good works to gain salvation and merit favour with a Holy God.

David's greatest difficulty—and it really irritated him—

was that salvation was apparently by faith alone and that all his so-called 'honest endeavours' were in vain. He read a book by one of the great preachers of the day, the Rev Stoddard, called *The Guide to Christ*, which helped him in some ways but not in others. Brainerd could not find out what faith was, nor what it was to believe and come to Christ, and in this vital aspect he found no help in Stoddard's book.

For months he struggled on; again and again he made renewed and valiant efforts to keep the law of God perfectly. Each time he fell back defeated by the unscalable heights of Mount Sinai, but every time he whipped himself up to make yet another vain attempt. A further point of perplexity and frustration was the sovereignty of God, and Romans chapter nine especially troubled him. He wrestled with these verses which somehow stirred an inner rebellion in his heart and an unwillingness to submit to a totally sovereign God. However, the Spirit of God was doing a deep work in his heart. He eventually came to see clearly that so far as pleasing God and salvation was concerned, all self-help was completely useless. Increasingly he realised that he was a sinner and alienated from the life of God.

David was fond of taking long walks in the woods around him, meditating and praying as he walked in solitary places. On the Sunday evening of July 12th, 1739 as he was walking in a thick dark grove, the light of God seemed to shine in his heart in a most marvellous way. He did not see an outward or physical light but the Spirit of God revealed to him in his heart and mind a vision of God such as he had never seen before. It was a view of God as such a perfect and wholly glorious and wonderful Being that made Brainerd just want to exalt Him and to gladly accept Him as Sovereign and King of the whole universe.

With this revelation of God came at last an understanding that salvation was entirely by the righteousness of Christ. The joy and sweetness of salvation welled up within his heart and for several days David was almost overwhelmed by the light of

God which made him see everything so differently. He was truly converted, born again of the Spirit of God, a new creature in Christ. There were still days when darkness and despair threatened to return but David Brainerd was irrevocably changed, his whole life was transfigured.

The desire to enter the ministry was no longer just a nice feeling but a call from God and in September he went to Yale College to further his studies. Just before he left for Yale he enjoyed another special time of great blessing when God met him very powerfully as he was praying. He was renewed and refreshed and furthermore the Spirit of God opened up the Bible to him in such a way that he knew by experience that it was indeed the Word of God. The blessing of that time remained with him throughout his first winter at Yale.

In January, however, there was a measles epidemic in the college and Brainerd caught the infection and went home to Haddam to recover. He was very ill for a few days but just before he went down with the sickness he had enjoyed another very special time of sweet refreshing from the Almighty as he was praying. For a little while he was seriously ill but God was so real to him at this time that all fear of death was removed, in fact he longed for it, so that he might be with Christ, rather than feared it. The crisis passed and soon David was fully recovered and able to resume his studies at the college. He studied hard and was ambitious to excel. In June, 1740, while taking one of his frequent 'prayer' walks, God again drew near to him in such a beautiful way that he was overwhelmed with the delight he found in His presence and found himself filled with love for all mankind and a longing that they should enjoy God in the same way. It was a foretaste of heaven, or so it seemed to him.

In the August of that same year Brainerd was studying so intensely that it began to affect his rather fragile health and the symptoms of tuberculosis began to show. Blood came up in his sputum and his tutor advised him to go home to recover. He desperately needed the rest as once again he stared death in the face and found himself reduced to a great weakness physically. But spiritually he grew stronger and by October he was enjoying deeper and closer communion with God than ever before. He was hungering and thirsting after God and His righteousness, and the Holy Spirit anointed him with a joy that lifted him into ecstasy. The love of God filled his eager heart. Physically he was recovered sufficiently to think of returning to college by the beginning of November, but he was so enjoying his special times of prayer that he was almost reluctant to return. However, return he did and the power of God rested upon him until the end of the year.

In January 1741, David became so engrossed in his studies that he felt his spiritual life was suffering adversely and that he had grown cold. The real truth was probably that he tended to be too introspective and a little over harsh with himself. After the 'mountain top' experiences he had enjoyed in the previous months, everyday life in college was bound to suffer by comparison. Happily his despondency was short-lived on this occasion because the Great Awakening, a revival which had begun in 1740 and in which George Whitefield played such an important role, reached Yale in February. The college was greatly affected and Brainerd was quickened and renewed.

During this visitation Brainerd and some of the other revived students began to meet together regularly for mutual encouragement and fellowship. They developed a relationship which enabled them to open themselves freely to each other. Their spiritual senses were heightened but they were still young and comparatively inexperienced and therefore tended to speak out bluntly on occasions. Revived believers inevitably make enemies as well as friends! Those still knowing nothing more than a nominal Christianity began to resent the fervour of their colleagues.

It so happened that after one of the tutors, a Mr Whittlesey, had led a gathering of the students in prayer, Brainerd and some of his group remained behind in the hall chatting together. The tutor's prayer had been very formal and lacking any real power. Before the revival had hit the college it probably would have passed without comment, but to this group who were on fire for God, it had to evoke some comment.

Thinking they were alone and engaged in private and personal conversation, one of them asked Brainerd what he thought of Whittlesey, to which he replied with a frankness typical of students at any university: 'He has no more grace than this chair'. A young freshman who was not actually in the hall but passing, chanced to overhear the remark and though he had not heard any name mentioned, he tittle-tattled it to a woman in the town and said that he thought Brainerd was saying this about one of the college rulers. She took it upon herself to inform the rector who sent for the freshman and extracted the full story from him including the names of all who were present. The rector then summoned those named to appear before him and bullied them into telling him of whom Brainerd had been speaking.

Brainerd was shattered when next he found himself forced to make a public confession before the whole college. This with rare courage he refused to do, feeling the unjustness of the treatment he was receiving. As the rector had already fined students for going to hear the great revival preacher, Mr Tennant in Milford, it was only too obvious that he was not in favour of the revival. Brainerd had also at some stage in the past supposedly made a remark about the rector's actions, namely that he wondered 'that the rector did not expect to drop down dead for fining students who had gone to hear Tennant'! Brainerd always maintained that he had no recollection of making this comment and it could not be proved. However, it was also brought up at this time and the unfortunate outcome was that David Brainerd was expelled from the college in the winter of 1742, during his third year there. It was a body blow, the unjustness of which he felt to his dying day, although he bore it manfully and with Christian grace. The disgrace to one as brilliant and sensitive as David was nevertheless an inward torture which left a deep scar. However, he eventually forgave those responsible and many came to feel that the blot was on Yale rather than on Brainerd.

It is interesting to note that the faculty of Yale College later had an acrimonious controversy with George Whitefield and clearly resented his forthright preaching of the gospel. In February 1745 the Yale Faculty made a formal declaration in which they accused Whitefield of saying that 'the generality of ministers are unconverted and unconverted ministers can no more be the means of any man's conversion than a dead man can beget living children'. This clearly reveals their attitude to the revival of those momentous days and it seems obvious that there was more to Brainerd's expulsion than first appears.

Shortly after his untimely and unwarranted expulsion from Yale, Brainerd went to live with Rev Mills at Ripton to carry on his studies for the ministry. In spite of his 'Gethsemane' experience he did not lose the spirit of prayer. He soon began again to enjoy great liberty in intercession and a great yearning for the salvation of the heathen came increasingly upon him. For some weeks, quite understandably, he had been deeply depressed about his future prospects in God's service, but the mountains of difficulty began to disappear as he prayed with growing power and liberty and he realised that if Christ chose to use and bless him, then it mattered little what man thought.

He spent a great deal of time in prayer and frequently set aside days for prayer and fasting. He loved to retire into the nearby woods for solitude and there, alone with God, he poured out his soul in earnest and intense intercession. More and more he found himself with a great burden for the conversion of the heathen. He drew near to God and God drew near to him in such a beautiful and inspiring way that he felt himself overwhelmed by the divine nearness. Such blessing made him so yearn over the unconverted that he agonised in prayer to the point where, even though he was in the shade and there was a cool breeze, he was covered in sweat.

In the middle of this period of much prayer Brainerd celebrated his twenty-fourth birthday on April 20th, 1742. At the end of the day he was able to write in his journal, 'This has been a sweet, happy day to me. I think my soul was never so drawn out in intercession for others, as it has been this night'. He was enabled to wrestle in prayer for his enemies and he renewed his vows of consecration to the Lord and His service, with a renewed determination and desire to wear out his life in God's service.

Prayer became Brainerd's priority and it was his joy to spend two hours at a time in secret prayer and communion with Christ. He loved to rise early in the morning and get alone with God to enjoy his presence. He thirsted for God, the living God, and he was not disappointed. His studies and preparations for ministry among the heathen became precious times as the Spirit of God gave him revelation and insight into the Word and into the things of God.

Occasionally he enjoyed fellowship with some of his Christian friends in Hartford but the sweetest fellowship of even his closest friends only left him with a greater longing for more retirement alone with Christ in prayer. That summer found him earnestly seeking the face of God for definite direction as to his future service and ministry. Mostly he found the Spirit of God greatly assisting him in these glorious times of prayer but even these 'high days' were interspersed with times of deadness and depression which left him despairing of ever achieving anything in God's service. At such times he was especially prone to sink to the deepest depths of melancholy as the memories of his disgrace in being expelled from Yale rose up before him. It was therefore a definite encouragement to him when, at the end of July, 1742, having travelled to Danbury, for examination by the Association as to his learning and experience regarding his fitness for the ministry, that he received a licence from them to preach the gospel. A godly ministerial friend prayed with him shortly afterwards and Brainerd resolved to devote himself entirely to God, for the rest of his days.

Next day Brainerd rode away from Danbury with a lighter heart and even as he journeyed prayer was a delight. He preached at Southbury and found that God was enabling him to touch hearts in a new way. Some two weeks later, however, on August 12th, he was so depressed that he despaired of ever becoming a missionary and for a little while thought his preaching was finished also. The people had, however, gathered and so he was more or less forced to preach and as he did so the Spirit of God came upon him both in prayer and preaching with the result that some of the local Indians present cried out in great distress as God convicted them.

Over the following weeks that pattern of times of special freedom in intercession and preaching, interspersed with fits of depression and discouragement, was repeated. Nevertheless Brainerd was growing spiritually all the time and on more than one occasion he experienced the nearness of heaven as never before. At the end of August as he was praying with one or two close friends he described this experience, saying, 'I think I scarce ever launched so far into the eternal world as then.' Prayer for the conversion of the heathen became an increasing burden but with it also came a growing assurance that God would do it and afford him a part in the accomplishing of it.

As autumn came so did new enjoyment of God's presence so that he could write privately in his diary (which he never showed to anyone else) 'O I love to live on the brink of eternity in my view and meditations. This gives me a sweet, awful and reverential sense and apprehension of God . . . .' Nevertheless, days of darkness when he was greatly depressed still occurred.

In the middle of November Brainerd received a letter inviting him to New York to discuss evangelism among the Indians with a group of ministers who represented a Scottish Missionary Society. He prayed about the invitation with two or three of his close friends and with a new peace in his heart he set off for that growing city. Although it was still extremely small compared with today, Brainerd found the noise and bustle most confusing. City life was not for him, he preferred the solitude of the forests where he could get alone with God. On the day of his appointment with the representatives of the Scottish Missionary Society he spent much time in prayer. They interviewed him and examined him on his studies in divinity and listened to him preach. It was quite an ordeal for David and he felt overwhelmed as he faced a sizeable congregation including some distinguished ministers. His own unworthiness so devastated him that he could scarcely preach, but though he felt he had done badly, these godly men obviously discerned his true spiritual worth. Quite sure he was just the man they were seeking for, they commissioned him to work among the Housatonic Indians at Kaunaumeek starting in the Spring of 1743.

In spite of his appointment, David rode away from New York with a dreadful feeling of inadequacy and spiritual inferiority. Even so he persisted in prayer for most of his thirty mile journey to White Plains. He was learning to pray without ceasing, his feelings of unworthiness only drove him to more prayer. In the next few weeks he visited his home town of Haddam once again. He had inherited some money from his father and while he was there his generous and unselfish spirit led him to sponsor a young man of promise to be educated and trained for the ministry.

Although David still suffered from days of depression he also continued to experience greater penetration and power in his times of prayer. He had plenty of opportunities to preach. He had many spiritual friends and it was his joy to share precious times of close fellowship and memorable times of prayer with them. At the beginning of February, 1743, he preached his farewell sermon and said his goodbyes to his friends as he prepared to set out on the first stages of his journey to the Indians, though he was due to spend a few more weeks on Long Island until winter passed. These he spent preparing himself by study and prayer for the task which lay ahead of him—to convert raw savages and bring them to a real saving experience of God's grace in Christ crucified.

It was a daunting prospect and it drove him to fervently seek God for the power of His Spirit to accomplish what was humanly impossible. April found him leaving the white settlement at Stockbridge and riding into the forest some twenty miles or so to a group of Indians at Kaunaumeek where he was to begin his work as a missionary. His first lodging was in a log cabin with a Scotsman, whose wife spoke almost no English. It was a very rough affair and David's bed consisted of some straw spread over boards, with a floor of bare earth. He frequently sought solitude in the surrounding forest and poured out his heart to God for his Christian friends now far away, and for the Indians in their dark paganism which now confronted him. He quickly realised that only a miracle from God could break this depressing, raw heathenism. On some days he found praying hard but at other times he experienced that it was 'sweet to pray' and found himself willing to undergo any suffering if only he could be used of God to bring people to know Christ as their Saviour.

His first efforts at preaching to the Indians were not very encouraging, although two or three showed some signs of concern, and one woman afterwards told him that her heart had cried ever since she first heard him preach. He persisted in prayer, rising early, and mostly retiring into the woods for privacy—his unsatisfactory lodging place providing him with but little of that commodity.

Almost three weeks after arriving there he celebrated his twenty-fifth birthday by setting it aside as a day of prayer and fasting. It turned out to be a celebration of the highest order for he recorded in his diary, 'God was with me of a truth. Oh, it was blessed company indeed! God enabled me to agonise in prayer so that I was quite wet with perspiration, though in the shade, and the wind cool. My soul was drawn out very much from the world, for multitudes of souls'. He felt that he wanted to wear out his life in the service of God and for His glory. Such times of prayer were by no means isolated occurrences. A few days after his birthday he rose early and for two hours prayed with such intensity that although it was a coolish day with but little sun he was soon perspiring freely.

These spiritual high days were intermingled with times of depression, but this was not surprising considering Brainerd's circumstances, being surrounded by a primitive race whose language he had not even begun to understand, and having to cope with very poor food, badly prepared, in his lodging place. After some weeks he left the log cabin to find out whether living with an Indian family in a wigwam would prove any better, but the smoke, coupled with the damp and cold soon began to get to him and his delicate health began to suffer. In spite of everything he soldiered bravely on, befriending the Indians and slowly winning their confidence. He stood up for them against some of the Dutch settlers who were laying claim to the area and driving them off their land, and for this action the Dutch hated him.

At the end of the following month, May, 1743 Brainerd journeyed to New Jersey to make arrangements for setting up a school among the Indians at Kanaumeek, with a very bright Indian who had become his interpreter, as the schoolmaster. This business satisfactorily accomplished, he journeyed for several more days to New Haven in the hope of achieving a reconciliation with his college, but this was never to be, and it saddened him deeply to his dying day.

On his return journey David got hopelessly lost and had to spend a night in the open. As well as being damp and cold, it was dangerous—wild animals and snakes thickly inhabiting the forests in those pioneering days. As always, he lifted his heart to God in prayer and proved His divine protection. The next day he found his way again and arrived on a Sunday in time to preach with greater power than ever before.

Finding that living in a wigwam was not the answer to his discomfort David started to build a little hut for himself. It was a real do-it-yourself affair, and with few tools available it was a long hard job. However, he was able to move into it at the end of July and found it much better, especially because he was now able to spend time inside in prayer, without interruption. This he did often and long, sometimes for a whole day. He found that the more he prayed the more easily he could pray and the more he wanted to.

Food was becoming a problem: David had to travel over ten miles to get bread and it was frequently mouldy and sour before he could eat it. Yet in spite of his poor health and miserable food, he enjoyed such great freedom in prayer that he praised God in all his circumstances and felt as rich as a king.

At the end of August, 1743, he took leave of his Indians to ride to New York and New Haven. At New Haven he met the great Jonathan Edwards for the first time. September 14th was the day when he should have received his degree at the college. To see his former classmates receiving their honours in the public ceremony was a severe test of his Christian character and humility—especially as, had it not been for the displeasure of the college governors, he would have been the head of the class. David shared his problem with Jonathan Edwards who was greatly impressed with the Christian spirit which he showed in the most trying circumstances. Influential friends of the Missionary Society David was serving, made earnest representation to the college authorities that David might have his degree conferred upon him. But in spite of this and David's having written a most humble letter of apology, the request was denied. They insisted that he would have to return to Yale for a further year for this to be possible, which David was unable to do, feeling so strongly his call to win the Indians for Christ. However, Jonathan Edwards bears witness that David showed no resentment or disappointment at this treatment, and David was enabled to pray with full forgiveness in his heart for all concerned. The will of God was all that mattered in his life and he was resolved that nothing should hinder his prayer life.

After having been delayed for about two weeks due to illness, David was able to return to his Indians at Kanaumeek on 4th October. They welcomed him back and he was pleased to find his little house safe and sound. He fell on his knees and thanked God for 'journeying mercies' once again. He quickly took up the burden of prayer and at the beginning of November he spent another whole day in prayer and fasting. On one occasion, as he read the story of Elijah he was much moved and cried out, 'Where is the Lord God of Elijah?' He felt inspired as he waited on God and was brought to see that God was still the same as in the days of Elijah. In prayer he wrestled with God, experiencing more liberty than for many months. Nothing seemed too hard for God to perform. His flagging hopes of seeing God work among the Indians were revived. He felt an overwhelming desire to see the power of God at work in conversion. He cried with Elisha of old for a double portion of that Spirit which was given to Elijah. A week later while again on his face before the Almighty during a day of prayer and fasting, David had the delightful experience of finding himself able to forgive and truly pray for those who had treated him wrongly.

Living alone in his little cottage spending much time in prayer was his joy and he found it irksome to have to break this pattern in order to take up the study of the Indian language with Rev John Sergeant, some twenty miles away at Stockbridge. The weeks he spent away from home in language study left him feeling out of touch with God. The journey through the woods in the depths of winter was a terrible ordeal and he had to undertake this on quite a number of occasions. Whenever he returned to his cottage he gave himself to prayer and soon the warm glow returned to his heart, so much so that he was reluctant to go to sleep and often continued seeking the face of God until midnight.

New Year's Day, 1744 discovered him engaged in earnest prayer and desiring to 'begin this year with God and spend the whole of it to His glory, either in life or death'. He rejoiced to find as he checked back that he had been able to give away for charitable purposes about one hundred pounds in the previous fifteen months. Before the first week of that year was out he set aside a whole day for fasting and prayer, neither eating nor drinking from evening to evening. He solemnly renewed his dedication to God as time seemed suddenly very short to him and eternity very near. Not content even with that devotion, the following day he spent in deep study, meditation and prayer.

Brainerd continued in very much the same vein throughout the first three months of 1744, not sparing himself in any way, desiring only to be used to win Indians for his Saviour. His aim was to communicate in the simplest possible way these great truths of the gospel which he judged best suited to bring about their speedy conversion. He exposed the sinfulness of sin but always made it clear that self-effort was of no use, and that their one and only hope lay in coming to Christ and trusting in His sufficiency. He composed simple prayers for them in their own language, as well as translating some of the psalms for them to sing. Matthew's gospel was expounded almost every evening when he was home. Such faithfulness did not go unrewarded and he was pleased with the progress many of these raw heathen made in his first year among them. His greatest delight was when his preaching to them was attended by the power of God, with the result that a few individuals were awakened to their need of Christ. Several of them came to him of their own accord, and some of them with tears, asked the great question, 'What shall we do to be saved?'

In March, having now completed almost a year at Kaunaumeek, he prayerfully considered the situation and felt the time had come for him to move further afield to other areas where the Indians were more numerous. Talking things through with the Indians and his friend Rev John Sergeant, the happy arrangement was agreed that the Indians would move their camp the twenty miles over to Stockbridge where Mr Sergeant would take them under his pastoral care.

David rode away from Kaunaumeek on the 14th March; travelling south-east he arrived two weeks later in New York. Soon after he proceeded to Elizabethtown where he met with the ministers of his missionary society. It was agreed that he should now go to the Delaware Indians. At this time he received invitations to at least two very attractive pastorates, but knowing only too well all the hardships involved, he resolutely set his face to return to his mission field among the Red Indians.

During April David enjoyed happy fellowship with his friends and relatives, but his health was not good. At the end of the month he said his farewells and set off for the Forks of Delaware. Travelling first to Stockbridge and then Kaunaumeek to dispose of his belongings there, he also used the opportunity to preach to the Indians he had influenced.

The journey to the Forks of Delaware lay to the far south-west and it proved to be an awful experience for him. He travelled some forty-five miles in driving rain along the east bank of the Hudson River to Fishkill, passing blood for much of the journey, such was the low state of his health. Nevertheless most of the time he was lifting up his heart in prayer for God to bless Delaware. Crossing the Hudson River he climbed to Goshen in the Highlands, and then rode another hundred miles through forests and territory which he described as 'desolate and hideous'.

Repeatedly rain-soaked, weak and weary with the journey, it was little wonder that when David arrived at a place just twelve miles north of the Forks of Delaware he was deeply depressed. Nor was there much to cheer him at first for the Indians were very scattered and the ones he did contact were antagonistic to Christianity because of the adverse behaviour of the white men they had met. The starkness of the Indians' heathenism was brought home to him when he attended one of their funerals and witnessed their pagan practices. He lifted his heart to God that their eyes might be opened to the truth, and when he was given the opportunity to preach, he found them very attentive.

The next day he had to undertake a further long journey to the south to Newark in New Jersey. Now it was the summer heat which plagued him and when he arrived at Newark where the Presbytery were met to effect his ordination, he was worn out. He had to preach in the afternoon and in spite of everything, God carried him through and afterwards he passed his examination before the Presbytery. Next morning (Tuesday, June 12th) he was further examined concerning his personal experience as a Christian, before being ordained. A week later he set off back on the three days' journey to the Forks of Delaware.

He immediately started preaching to the Indians but it quickly became clear to him that hopes of reaching them were as dark as midnight, unless God moved upon them by His Spirit. Repeatedly he retired into solitary places in the forest to give himself to intercession for them. As he rode to where they were, he was constantly engaged in supplication, so that when he preached he found his heart filled with the love of God for them and he rejoiced to find them listening intently. As he rode away his prayers were mingled profusely with praise for this encouraging sign.

Physically Brainerd was in a terribly weak state, but spiritually he declared 'I felt abundant strength in the inner man'. His overwhelming desire now was for the conversion of the Indians. Days of prayer were the order rather than the exception, and (after one such day) when he learned that there was to be idolatrous feast and dance the next day, he resolved to do his utmost to break it up. On his knees he was in such an anguish of soul for the Indians that the sweat ran down his face and body. He was lifted up into such a place with God that he felt that he cared not where or how he lived, or what hardships he went through so that he could gain souls to

Christ. When he slept, it was only to dream about their conversion, and immediately he woke up his first thought was of this spiritual warfare of God against Satan.

The Indians' frolic was scheduled for Sunday, July 22nd, and as he rode to the appointed place David prayed without ceasing. They had started by the time he arrived but such was his presence that he succeeded in getting them to stop and listen to him preach. He was disappointed that there did not seem much of a response from them, and in the afternoon he preached again with more force, but still without the response for which he was hoping. As he left he felt that Satan was taunting him that his task was hopeless. He resisted this suggestion and determined to continue to wait upon God for their salvation.

In spite of experiencing much sickness, pain and weakness throughout this summer of 1744, Brainerd steadfastly continued with his preaching and praying. Discovering that some of the Indians were afraid to embrace Christianity through fear of being bewitched by the medicine men, he boldly and openly challenged these powers of darkness to do their worst upon him first. It was a most effective demonstration of the power of Christ to keep from evil.

At the beginning of October, accompanied by another white man, two Indian chiefs and an interpreter, David set off to travel west to reach the Susquehannah Indians. He soon discovered that this journey was far worse than anything he had encountered before. They climbed over steep mountains, and then plunged down into deep ravines; they struggled through swamps and clambered over rocks. In the process one evening his horse broke its leg and fell under him. Fortunately he was not hurt but the horse had to be put out of its misery, and David was forced to continue on foot.

Eventually they arrived at the Susquehannah River and found a small group of Indians who willingly listened to David preach. After a few days they pushed on further. The territory was hostile, winter was coming on, and prayer for protection was made from heartfelt intercession as in the darkness of night they heard wolves howling around them.

It was a relief to return to the place which he had made his base at the Forks of Delaware. With the advent of winter it was imperative to erect a proper shelter, which, with the help of the Indians, David was able to do. Throughout November and December he continued to preach whenever possible, seizing every opportunity to reach the Indians for Christ. He prayed much in secret and was very conscious on many occasions that God was helping him. The man who was now acting as his interpreter was not a Christian, but as David preached and he interpreted time after time, the message began to affect him. David sensed this and spent a day in prayer and fasting for his conversion and for three or four others who were under conviction. As David preached on December 18th God so blessed him that a very old man, whom he supposed was possibly a hundred years old, was so affected that he wept. The interpreter was also greatly moved and the following days it was clear that he was a changed person.

David finished the year of 1744 in a low state of health, but in quite high spirits as he saw the evidence of God at work among his beloved Indians.

The beginning of what was to prove to be the most memorable year of his life found David, as ever, on his knees. January 3rd, 1745, he set aside as yet another day of prayer and fasting seeking God for an outpouring of His Spirit upon himself, his Indians, and the church of God in general. During the first weeks of this year as he waited before God he became conscious that he had fallen into the common trap of seeking holiness in his own strength, now God revealed to him that this too was only possible by His grace and strength. The invitation of Jesus in John 7: 37 became increasingly precious to him at this time: 'Jesus stood and cried, saying "If any man thirst, let him come unto Me and drink." ' He found himself longing to proclaim such grace to the whole world of sinners.

On Sunday February 17th, he preached on this text to a quite large gathering of white people, some of them travelling thirty miles to hear him. He spoke to them morning, afternoon, and evening from this one text, experiencing greater liberty than ever before in proclaiming God's free grace to lost sinners. It was a remarkable day with many in tears and more still under conviction. David was full of joy at the end of that great day.

With the coming of spring David felt he had to make plans to enable him to return to the Indians on the Susquehannah River. With this in mind, at the beginning of March he set off on a journey to New England to visit ministers and Christian friends there, with the hope of raising support for a colleague to join him in the work. The experience of having been very much alone for two years was beginning to affect him. The journey to New England involved him in a round trip of some six hundred miles on horseback, and took him five weeks. Although he was very weary from this long journey within a few days David travelled to Philadelphia to obtain permission from the governor to live at Susquehannah among the Indians. Not surprisingly when he finally got back to his little home at the Forks of Delaware he was quite ill for several days and had to take to his bed to rest. Although still weak and somewhat dreading the fearful journey which he knew lay ahead of him to Susquehannah, on the 8th of May he set out with his interpreter. All too soon his worst fears were realised—on the second day of their journey they ran into a great rainstorm. It was impossible to light a fire and there was no shelter as they pushed bravely on. To their dismay they found their horses so weakened through eating a poisonous plant that they had to dismount and proceed on foot. They were drenched to the skin and buffeted mercilessly by a fierce north-easterly wind. Fortunately they came across a bark hut just before nightfall—without its shelter they felt they could not have survived through the night.

When they finally reached the Susquehannah River they left their horses and travelled for a hundred miles down the river by canoe. En route they stopped and preached at many Indian settlements by the river and David found most of them ready to listen to his preaching. It was rough going; the Indian canoes were made of very thin birch bark which made them light enough to be carried easily when some waterfall was confronted, but did not make for relaxing travel! The Indians were experts when it came to shooting the rapids or guiding their fragile crafts through the dangerous rocks, providing David with more than a few heart-stopping moments during the two weeks they spent on the river.

On David's return journey to the Forks of Delaware as he was riding through the terrible terrain he was seized with a burning fever and began to pass blood. He had to rest in an Indian trader's hut for a week before he was able to continue his difficult ride back to his little home. Once back, in spite of his low state of health, he could not refrain from preaching. He travelled some fifty miles to Neshaminy, to share ministry with Mr Beatty at his meeting house. On the Sunday as they celebrated the Lord's supper, a crowd of some three to four thousand gathered, and as David preached extemporaneously from Isaiah 53: 10, 'Yet it pleased the Lord to bruise him', God greatly blessed his ministry and hundreds were deeply affected. It was a foretaste of the revival soon to break.

Having now spent a year at the Forks of Delaware in Pennsylvania, which included two journeys to the Susquehannah Indians, feeling some disappointment over the small results, and hearing about some more Indians at a place called Crossweeksung, he determined to visit them. (Unknown to David his ministry was bearing more fruit than he realised. Quite a number of Susquehannah Indians had forsaken their idol worship and this news had spread through the great forests.)

He arrived at Crossweeksung in the third week of June but was disappointed to find only two or three families there. After preaching to them, however, he was encouraged when he discovered the women hurrying off to tell their friends some ten to fifteen miles away that the preacher had arrived. Daily the numbers grew. Starting with just seven or eight, soon there were thirty—all listening with great intensity. The thirty became forty, and still they came. Now they were hungry to hear more and they asked David to preach twice a day. On the first of July he spoke to around fifty Indians and he was amazed to find how much of the truth they had received and retained. The next day when he told them that he must leave them for a while and return to the Forks of Delaware, they were very sad but eager for him to return and promised of their own accord that they would all regather with as many of their friends as possible and live together so as to get the most out of another visit. Some of them were in tears and showed great concern for their salvation.

No sooner was Brainerd back at the Forks of Delaware than he was preaching again, and he was thrilled to find the people there responding to the Word of God, so much so that many of the Indians wept through the whole of the service. A week later (on Sunday 21st July), he was deeply moved when the interpreter and his wife publicly confessed their faith in Christ by baptism. This interpreter had been with David during the time he had been at the Forks of Delaware, which was about a year. His name was Moses Tinda Tautamy. When he first worked with David he was a hard drinker and though well equipped in the Indian and English languages, he was ignorant of true Christianity, which made things difficult for David who had to do all his preaching through him. Gradually, however, the truth of David's preaching and life began to affect the interpreter. In several of the services when the Spirit of God was moving with power, he was clearly affected. Finally, after a period of deep conviction in which he knew that he was lost without Christ and could never by any means save himself, God spoke clearly into his heart and it was soon evident to David and to all that he had been born again. Immediately there was a difference in the way he interpreted. There was a new rapport between them and

Moses seemed to have the same anointing and expressions as David himself. Furthermore, frequently when David had finished preaching, Moses would carry on preaching himself and exhorting his fellow Indians to come to Christ!

David was eager to return to the Indians at Crossweeksung where he had been so conscious that the Spirit of God was at work, and the beginning of August found him back there. Nor was he disappointed, he was gratified to discover the Indians even more keen to hear the Word of God. When he left them in June he had put them in contact with another faithful servant of God in the vicinity, Rev William Tennent, and his ministry had been very profitable to them. What a change he found in them in such a short time. Now they would not begin a meal until David arrived to say grace; they wept to think that previously they had eaten in honour of devils and never given thanks to God for their food. August 3rd, 4th, 5th, 6th and 7th were all precious days. It was a joy to preach to them, and again he could not resist from returning to one of his favourite texts: 'Jesus stood and cried, saying "If any man thirst let him come unto me and drink" '. John 7: 37. Tears flowed freely and a great spirit of Christian love was evident among them.

But August 8th was the day of days. By now almost seventy Indians had assembled, some of them travelling from before dawn to join them. In the afternoon of that never-to-be-forgotten day, as David was speaking from Luke 14: 16–23 (the parable of the great supper) it was soon very clear to him that something unusual was happing—the Word of God was having a visible effect upon his hearers. But it was when he had finished his sermon and was speaking individually to some of these who were obviously under deep conviction, that suddenly, as on the Day of Pentecost, the power of God seemed to come down upon them all like a rushing almighty wind with astonishing energy and bore down everyone before it. David stood amazed at this demonstration of the power of God. He could only compare it to the irresistible force of great torrents of water such as he had experienced when travelling down the mighty rapids. This power swept everything before it. Old and young were equally affected. Drunken wretches of many years and little children of six and seven were all crying to God for mercy and forgiveness. The most stubborn were now forced to bend before the power of God. A leading Indian who was very proud and most self-righteous and who felt superior to the others because he knew more, and claimed to have been a Christian for ten years, was now humbled and weeping bitterly before God. Another old man who had been a murderer, a medicine man (or conjurer, a pow-pow), and a chronic drunkard, was also reduced to tears and made to cry to God for mercy. It seemed to David that everyone was praying and crying for mercy in every part of the building in which the meeting had taken place, as well as many outside. Many were unable to move or stand, they were prostrated under the power of God. No one seemed aware of anyone but themselves.

Some of the white people who had come along more out of curiosity than real interest in God's Word, were also affected in the same way and under deep conviction of sin were crying to God for forgiveness.

An Indian woman who had also come to mock was so deeply affected that she could neither sit nor stand without people holding her, nor could she move. Afterwards she lay flat on the ground praying earnestly, ignoring everyone around her. For hours she lay there crying, 'Have mercy on me and help me give you my heart'.

However, there was never any attempt whatsoever on Brainerd's part to induce such fear as occurred. He did not harangue them with the terrors of hell, but to the contrary, he found that the great awakening with its attendant manifestation of the power of God, came when he was exalting the compassion of a dying Saviour, and the free offers of God's grace to needy sinners.

It was indeed a day of God's power and David felt that it was enough to convince even an atheist of the truth and power of God's Word. The countless hours spent in praying and fasting, his faithfulness in spite of physical weakness and having to endure the most terrible hardships, his persistent unwearying preaching and testifying in season and out of season, were now rewarded openly. The break he had longed and yearned for came at last. The fire of the Lord fell. David's prayer for a double portion of God's Spirit was dramatically answered. The remarkable thing was that all this happened at a time when he confessed that his hopes were at their very lowest and was entertaining serious thoughts of giving up his mission among the Indians!

This marvellous season of blessing continued throughout August. Indians who but shortly before this were hallooing and yelling in their idolatrous feasts and drunken frolics, were now transformed by the power of God. Love reigned among them. This new affection between the newly awakened believers made such an impression on the other Indians that they wanted the same love and joy so much that they were reduced to tears. The light of God shone from the faces of these new converts. There were cases of conviction daily. Old men were affected and melted to tears and made to cry out aloud and to groan under the burden of their sins. One said that it seemed to him that all the sins of his lifetime had been committed but yesterday. Broken marriages were restored. Drunkenness, their most besetting sin, almost disappeared completely.

At the end of August Brainerd felt that it was his duty to return to the Indians at Susquehannah. Before he left Crossweeksung (and there were now some ninety-five Indians, old and young, nearly all of whom were filled with joy in the Lord Jesus) he asked them to pray for his visit to Susquehannah. When he rode away on his horse there was about an hour and a half of daylight remaining. The Indians immediately began praying and they continued praying virtually all night. Yet such was the blessing of God upon these new converts that they could hardly believe that it was nearly morning when they finally stopped praying.

On his way to Susquehannah David made it his business to visit the Forks of Delaware again and when he preached there on the 1st of September, a Sunday, his word was again with power and was blessed to gatherings of whites as well as the redskins. Over the next nine days as he preached, God's presence again became very real and quite a number of the most unlikely people—both white and red—were affected and reduced to tears, with many crying out aloud under the convicting power of God's Spirit.

Proceeding on his journey he next called at Shaumoking, over a hundred miles away. The three different tribes of Indians here were reckoned to be the most drunken and depraved in the whole region, and it seemed to David that it was very much a centre of Satan's dark power. He stayed for several days and managed to get a hearing from some fifty of them who were sober, and before he left he experienced great freedom in prayer as he sought God on their behalf and believed that Satan's power would soon be broken there by the power of Christ.

Forty miles or so downriver David called at a large inhabited island called Juncauta, which he had visited the previous spring. His visit coincided with a great heathen sacrifice and dance they were planning for the following day. He was saddened by all that he saw as they danced and whooped around their great bonfire, which continued all night. It was with a sad heart that he left with them unwilling to give him a hearing. He was more aware than ever that they were indeed Satan's captives and that only the power of God would ever change them.

When he returned to Crossweeksung at the beginning of October he could not help but notice the contrast between the changed lives of the new Christians and those still in the grip of heathenism that he had just left. It was a great joy for him to be once again preaching to those who were so responsive to the gospel. There was scarcely a dry eye among them and even when he retired to sleep, many of them continued praying among themselves for another two hours. The blessing continued to flow throughout October and David was lifted up to see the reality of the change wrought by the gospel of God's love; it made him feel that all his sufferings, his days and nights of praying, were more than worthwhile. He found it remarkable that as soon as new Indians joined the gatherings they were immediately affected and brought under conviction and concern for their souls. Although there were remarkable demonstrations of the power of God, such as groaning with intensity of their repentance, and some prostrations, with many crying out loud for mercy, yet there was nothing of wild fanaticism, and no convulsions or screaming. There was only one possible explanation—Almighty God was at work by His Spirit. Many were delivered permanently from drunkenness, thieves were made honest, debts were repaid and love reigned supreme. The grasp of doctrine by the new converts amazed him, he felt that they had received and grasped so much doctrine in the space of just a few short months which normally would have taken years to instill.

As well as preaching to groups both large and small, David also spent a lot of time going from wigwam to wigwam and instructing them individually. His dedication was total, his devotion complete. Many times he was kept busy dealing with inquirers both day and night. This continued with but little abatement to the end of that memorable year of 1745. On the last Sunday of the year (December 29th) as he preached, many white people as well as Indians were in tears, and after the service many followed to his house and asked with tears in their eyes, what they must do to be saved. As he spoke to them, once again the Spirit of God came upon them in such power that the house was soon filled with their cries and groans.After what he had seen David felt that he would never despair again of any man or woman, no matter how hard a case; Christ was more than sufficient for their need and able to save them to the uttermost.

The New Year of 1746 saw him catechising these new converts and doing his utmost to ensure that they were well grounded in the great truths. Even at such times of solid teaching, the Spirit of God would suddenly break in upon them in a remarkable and unexpected way. It was true revival.

On February 1st, an old conjurer (or medicine man) who had kept many back from coming to Christ by his influence among the Indians as a magician of repute, after a long period of resisting God's Spirit, finally yielded himself fully to Christ. It was a great and notable victory. This man had been a drunkard as well as a much feared 'magic man' dealing and dabbling in Satanic arts, and he was also a murderer. That day, however, as David was catechising in his usual manner in the evening, God so dealt with this evil man that he felt he was literally dropping into hell and he trembled for many hours, before finding peace in Christ and forgiveness. After this he followed David everywhere and when another medicine man threatened to put a spell on David, the converted conjurer boldly withstood him and told him he could not do that and shared his testimony, how that he had once been just as powerful as this man but as soon as he had come to Christ all the power of evil spirits in his life had left him for good.

The spring of 1746 saw a wonderful church of converted Indians established. There were now around 150 living at Crossweeksung and in April they celebrated communion for the first time. It was a great occasion. The change that God had made in these raw heathens in the space of just nine months was remarkable; before they were always quarrelling and fighting, now a spirit of love and peace prevailed.

In the summer David asked his group of new believers at Crossweeksung to pray for him as once again he set off to visit the Susquehannah. This time he took six of his new converts with him which proved to be a wise move. His own health was rapidly deteriorating and he refused to spare himself in any way. He still set himself aside to spend days of praying and fasting and spiritually he was in perfect health, although no doubt because of his low state of physical health he suffered from times of depression.

In mid-August David arrived again at Shaumoking where he had preached the previous year, and this time he was given more of a hearing. After he had preached to a large number of Indians, the six new converts reinforced his message by their testimonies. It proved very effective. David's visit to the Susquehannah Indians on this occasion was much more encouraging than his earlier ones, and many of the local Indians travelled with his party through the forests in order to hear him preach again.

He returned home to his Indians at Crossweeksung at the end of September. He was glad to be back with them and they were thrilled to see him again and to hear how God had answered their prayers on his behalf on this last trip. But it was only too apparent that David was now seriously ill. He was frequently coughing blood and suffering with a burning fever. David was very conscious that time was running out for him and he was very anxious to have another communion service. This was planned for the first Sunday in October. The Indians at Forks of Delaware were notified of this (some forty-seven of whom had now made a good profession of faith in Christ) and some of them were able to make the journey to Crossweeksung. Though very weak David somehow managed to preach and give communion to some forty Indians, as well as to some very dear white believers. God's presence was powerfully present, many felt their hearts melted before Him and two made a public profession of faith. But by the end of the day poor David could scarcely make it to his house which was close-by and had to be helped by his friends. He was very poorly for the remainder of October, and he was distressed at the beginning of November when he found he was still too weak to preach. He managed to ride to Elizabethtown where some of his friends cared for him but such was the low state of his health that he had to stay there for four months.

With the approach of spring in 1747 David summoned up

all his strength and with great difficulty managed to make a final visit to his greatly loved Indian congregation at Crossweeksung. It was the last time he was able to be with them and the parting was one of many tears and much sadness.

It had been known for some time that David had tuberculosis but the doctor now had to tell him that it was a terminal case and that there was nothing that could be done for him. The only advice they could proffer was for him to do some riding whenever he could manage it. His brother John came to visit David in Elizabethtown and it was a great comfort and relief to David that John was willing and able to take care of the Indians at Crossweeksung.

Shortly after his twenty-ninth birthday on the 20th April 1747, David left New Jersey and travelled slowly to New York and then north to his home town of East Haddam. He was too ill to attend public worship but he found great delight even in his sufferings in secret prayer. God's presence was so wonderfully revealed to him on more than one occasion as he lay in his bed, that he just longed to be in heaven with his Saviour.

At the end of May he somehow summoned up enough strength to ride on to Northampton, in Massachusetts, to the home of the renowned Jonathan Edwards. This was a double delight to David partly because Northampton had been the scene of revival ever since 1734, and also because David had become engaged to Edwards' young daughter, Jerusha, in whom he found a kindred spirit. During his last months it was the charming and gentle Jerusha who was his constant companion and nurse. She travelled with him to Boston on June 9th, but the journey took its toll and on June 18th David was desperately ill and was at death's door for a time.

He was able to return to Northampton but physically he continued to decline and September 17th was the last day he was able to leave his sickroom. Constantly he prayed for Christ's Kingdom to flourish and he was especially concerned for the outpouring of God's Spirit upon all ministers of the gospel. He talked openly of his coming death but far from fearing it he was eagerly anticipating it and called it 'that glorious day'. On September 29th two young men who were his friends and also candidates for the ministry were allowed to see David and he exhorted them as a dying man to especially concentrate on prayer and fasting as a key to success in the work of God, as he himself had proved.

By now he was too weak to even sit up in bed and on the 4th of October he very tenderly told his dear Jerusha that he was willing even to part from her but only because he knew that they would be reunited for a happy eternity together. (Little did he realise it but within four months, young Jerusha was taken ill and after a short five-day illness in February 1748, she died in her eighteenth year.) On the night of October 8th David was in great pain and as dawn approached on Friday, he was finally released from his sufferings at about 6.00 am. His body was laid to rest at Northampton, on the Monday following. It was an occasion that none of the great crowd of mourners would ever forget.

Jonathan Edwards left it on record that he and his family counted it the greatest privilege and honour to have had such an outstanding servant of God in their home. His dying words, prayers and counsels, and his triumphant death, made an indelible impression upon them all. Nearly two hundred and fifty years later his life is still stirring and challenging the church.

Brainerd once wrote in his diary, 'I longed to be a flame of fire continually glowing in the divine service and building up Christ's kingdom to my last and dying breath'. That prayer was abundantly answered.

5: Madame Guyon

The French countryside around the estate of the wealthy de La Mothe family in the Province of Orelanais was looking very beautiful in the Spring of 1648. Seigneur (or Lord) Claude Bouvieres de La Mothe was well satisfied with life. In addition to his family title he carried the prestigious position of mayor of Montargis. His second marriage was going well. He already had a son and daughter from his first marriage; his new wife also had a daughter from a previous union and now she was eight months pregnant. God had been good to him and as a pious Catholic he faithfully attended mass and was genuinely grateful for his many blessings. Suddenly his peace was shattered: one of the servants burst in on him with the news that his wife had accidentally been badly frightened and it had brought on premature labour. She was already giving birth to the baby and the signs were not good. Praying fervently as he went to investigate, Seigneur Claude found his usually well-run household in a state of panic. His wife's condition was poor although the midwife was reassuring, but the premature baby girl was a very feeble little thing and not expected to survive. He rushed to bring the priest to baptise it but by the time he returned with him the child had to all intents stopped breathing. After frantic efforts, however, signs of life appeared again. It was touch and go for several days and more than a month passed before the priest was able to baptise the delicate Jeanne Marie Bouvieres de La Mothe.

Throughout the first two and a half years of her life baby Jeanne was weak and sickly and required a lot of care, which her mother was not willing to give having a distinct aversion to girls. Seigneur Claude sensed this and when she was two-and-a-half years old he decided that it would be best for everyone if she was placed in the tender care of nuns in the nearby Ursuline Seminary. He was very fond of his fragile but pretty little daughter.

The nuns took to this precocious toddler and cared for her very tenderly but after six months Seigneur Claude decided to bring her home. Unfortunately his wife did not seem any more inclined to give her little daughter the motherly care and affection she needed and deserved. Jeanne Marie was mostly left to the servants and her stepbrother and stepsisters. The boy being much older loved to boss her around and to tease her. In spite of not being very strong Jeanne Marie was very lively and got into more than her fair share of scrapes. Several times she fell down into quite a deep cellar in which the firewood was stored only to escape unhurt.

When Jeanne Marie was four the Duchess of Montbason, a family friend, came to the Benedictine Convent and persuaded Seigneur Claude to enroll her there. The Duchess took special care of this little treasure of a girl who was showing herself to be very bright indeed. She followed the great lady round like her shadow. The religious atmosphere seemed to suit her and she was highly delighted when they made a special nun's habit for her to wear. She soaked up the ceremonial worship in the chapel services and took the instruction very seriously. The atmosphere was quite strict, in keeping with such an establishment, and one night little five-year-old Jeanne Marie had a frightening dream of hell: she was so afraid that she refused to close her eyes again until she had made her confession. She was too young to confess alone and so a nun accompanied her to the priest to whom she made a lengthy confession. They were both taken aback when she announced that she had some doubts about the Catholic faith and Church, but she admitted that she now really did believe in hell! Although both the priest and the nun smiled at such things coming from one so young they recognised the sincerity and unusual understanding she showed. It was also clear that she already realised that she was a sinner and in need of salvation.

Understandably the older girls in the convent school were a little jealous of this extremely pretty and very religious tiny tot who was the Duchess's special favourite. Furthermore, Jeanne Marie was not slow to share her 'religious experiences' openly with them all, which only served to provoke them against her. She was so simple and unaffectedly childish that she did not realise that the older girls were laughing at her behind her back. One day she startled them all by declaring that she had a desire to become a martyr—she was so serious about it all that the girls decided to go along with her in helping her on the road to martyrdom. To the older girls it was all a bit of a giggle, mixed undoubtedly with a little bit of envy.

After her confession Jeanne Marie had a nice warm glow in her tiny heart and she began to spend longer times in prayer than the other girls. She took them seriously when they said that as a martyr she would go straight to heaven. When the girls told her they had fixed the day of her martyrdom she was very excited and told them she would be ready. The girls spread a red cloth on the floor and one of them got hold of a real sword. They called the prospective martyr into the room, all of them anxious to see just how far this little religious martyr would go. Jeanne Marie came in, her little face aglow. In her childish mind she had somehow got the idea that she could become a martyr without really dying. To her it was pretending but in a very real way, and she was determined to go through with it and face her ordeal with courage.

The girls made her kneel down in the middle of the red cloth and then joined in as she recited the creed in a trembling, pipy voice. She clutched her rosary tightly to her and prayed with her eyes closed. One of the big girls then took the sword and raised it high over the kneeling figure. As a deathly hush descended upon the room, Jeanne Marie opened her tear-filled eyes and saw the sword. For the first time real fear seized her; suddenly it was all for real and she panicked. 'Wait! Hold on!' she cried, 'It is not right that I should die without getting my father's permission.' Her frightened words broke the spell and the older girls jeered at her and taunted her. They told her that she had lost her chance of martyrdom for ever; now she was lost, hell awaited her. Bewildered as she was, it at last dawned on her that the girls had just used her for their own entertainment; to them it was all a rather malicious spoof to show her up as a coward and a hypocrite. She wept in dismay and fled, deeply disturbed and upset. She really believed what the girls said, that she had lost her chance of going to heaven and forfeited all chance of martyrdom. The Duchess, the nuns, the priest, and finally her father, all tried to comfort her but in vain. Depressed and sick she eventually had to be taken home and it took a full year for her to recover from the incident.

By the time Jeanne Marie was seven her father decided that it was safe for her to return to the Ursuline Seminary for schooling. Her two step-sisters had become teaching-nuns there and he especially requested that she be placed under the care of the older daughter who had grown very close to Jeanne Marie. It was a happy arrangement and Jeanne Marie made rapid progress under her sister's tuition. She benefited too from the older girl's religious devotion. When she was eight she was brought home by her father to meet a very special guest, Queen Henrietta Maria of England, the daughter of Henry IV and sister of King Louis XIII of France. Queen Henrietta had been living in France in exile for twelve years, hoping that she might yet be restored to the throne if the political climate changed. Jeanne Marie made an immediate impression upon the Queen with her dances and recitations, and by her charming and polite mannerisms. Above all she captivated the Queen and the chaplain with her unusually wise answers to difficult religious questions they plied her with. The Queen was so taken with the child that she wanted her as a personal Maid of Honour for her daughter. Jeanne

Marie's heart leapt at the prospect. However, her father politely but firmly declined.

Back at the convent school Jeanne Marie's religious inclinations once again came to the fore. She loved to steal away alone into the garden chapel and pray in secret. Sometimes she spent hours on her knees with her rosary and prayer book. The nuns observed her devoutness but were a little anxious when she appeared paler than usual. She appeared to be eating her food regularly. Every morning she would take her breakfast plate and then march to the garden chapel to pray. Only when the chapel was given an extra clean was it discovered that she had been fasting. Behind the statue of the Christ-child they found a pile of food from many uneaten breakfasts! The nuns lovingly and kindly remonstrated with her: the child was very delicate and they were concerned for her health. Their fears proved only too well founded for when she was nine she suffered a very severe haemorrhage and they feared for her life. She recovered but remained a sickly child.

Life was not easy for Jeanne Marie. When she was at home she found that it was impossible for her to please her mother no matter how hard she tried. Her mother's affections were all showered upon the son. When she was back at the convent the younger stepsister decided that she should have a share in teaching Jeanne Marie. She was a less able teacher, and jealous and frequently she whipped her little charge. Their father ultimately learned what was happening and at ten years of age Jeanne Marie found herself back home once more, but it was not for long. True to form, after a visit from the Prioress of the Dominicans, Seigneur Claude decided that *this* was the place for his daughter. The Prioress gave him her personal assurance that she would look after his precious daughter as though she were her own child, and for a time she held to her promise. She kept her constantly with her and tutored her personally; Jeanne Marie made rapid progress for she was a bright girl and teachable. Unfortunately this did not last very long; changes in the convent made it impossible for the Prioress to continue to devote so much time to her and she was frequently left on her own and unsupervised. Then Jeanne Marie caught chicken pox and was quarantined in her room with only a lay-sister to bring her food. However, Jeanne Marie was a keen reader and she was delighted to discover a Bible in the sickbay. Left to her own devices on the long lonely days of her sickness she devoured this wonderful book. She read it from morning to evening, day after day, chapter after chapter, book after book; she immersed herself in it during the three weeks of her illness.

After only eight months she was brought home once more; her father ever living in hopes that his wife would have more patience with his favourite daughter now that she was older. But no, everything was just the same. It was alright for Jeanne Marie when her father was around at weekends, but when he was away there was quarrelling among the children, and Madame de La Mothe, though a good woman in some ways and given to charitable works among the poor in the neighbourhood, just could not get on with Jeanne Marie. The son was her spoilt favourite and he exploited the situation to make Jeanne Marie's life as miserable as possible.

When she was nearly twelve she took her first communion. Her favourite and devoted stepsister prepared her thoroughly for this during the weeks of Lent. (Seigneur Claude observing his daughter suddenly developing into a tall and exceedingly attractive girl had decided that she would be able to cope with returning to the Ursuline Convent yet again.) Jeanne Marie celebrated the eucharist at Easter with great joy and decided that more than anything else she wanted to be a nun. Soon the jealous younger stepsister intervened again and insisted that she had a share in teaching Jeanne Marie, with the result that the poor girl found herself pulled in opposite directions, resulting in a quick relapse of her religious aspirations.

Now that Jeanne Marie was blossoming into a truly beautiful young lady her mother at last began to take an interest in her—even if it was only to dress her up and show her off in her elevated circle of society. Though only twelve years old a number of eligible young men wanted to marry her, proposals which were immediately rejected by her father. But the effect of such attention upon the child was not good and understandably it went to her head. She spent a long time admiring herself in the mirror, and at the high society parties many men gave her long and adoring glances. This continued for quite some time until one day she learned that one of her cousins, Monsieur De Toissi, was leaving to take up missionary work in China. Such a sacrifice stopped Jeanne Marie in her pretty tracks and challenged her to renew her desires to serve God also. She poured out her heart to her confessor-priest which gave her some relief but not the enlightenment she really needed. She redoubled her efforts to gain salvation by her own merit and became very religious once again.

For long periods during her early teens the girl shut herself away to seek God as best she knew how. She fasted, prayed, studied the Bible and read some of the great devotional classics such as Thomas à Kempis' *Imitation of Christ*, Francis de Sales' books, and *The life of Madame de Chantal*. From her reading she glimpsed that there were other forms of prayer than reciting the written ones and she asked her priest to teach her but he had no idea what she was talking about. She pursued her task with amazing fortitude for one so young. Having read that Madame de Chantal had branded the name of Jesus with a hot iron over her heart she tried to emulate her. She knew her parents would never allow her to go so far but she opted to write the name of Jesus on paper, and then with ribbons, thread and needle she sewed it to her skin in four places. This painful penance she carried around under her clothes for quite some time. She practised many austerities in her endeavour to find salvation but all in vain. She sought it by good works, feeding the poor, giving everything she had to clothe them. When her parents were out she would bring the poor home and serve them herself.

Her consuming desire was to become a nun but her father was adamantly against it. Knowing her parents would never give their consent she stole away secretly on one occasion to the Convent of Saint Francis de Sales and begged them to receive her into their order. But she was still very young and they dared not admit her without her parents' consent. It was all very frustrating and disappointing and after about a year of this her religious zeal began to wane. In this unhappy state of mind Jeanne met and fell in love with an attractive young cousin of hers. He was religiously inclined and the attraction was mutually fervent. She was as head over heels in love as only a fourteen-year-old girl can be when she falls into that blissful state for the first time. Life was suddenly wonderful but she was doomed to disappointment. Being close blood-relatives, marriage was out of the question and so ended what was probably her first and last true love. She tried to forget him but it all left her a very mixed-up young girl.

In 1663 the de La Mothe family moved to Paris, which under the young and ambitious twenty-four year old King Louis XIV was reaching new heights of extravagance and fashion. This was much to the taste of Madame de La Mothe who revelled in being a part of the rapidly expanding royal court. Paris was the place to be: as well as a fast-moving, pleasure-loving city, it was also the great centre of science and literature. At fifteen, Jeanne Marie had developed into a tall, well-proportioned, French beauty. Her beautiful complexion, sparkling eyes, dark hair, and round face, were guaranteed to turn heads even in that elevated society and Madame de La Mothe exploited it for her own advantage. She basked in the reflected glory of her daughter as they moved around not only in Paris but at the increasingly splendid royal palace at Versailles, upon which young King Louis was lavishing his attention. It was all too much for young Jeanne Marie and it swept her off her feet. Finding herself the centre of attraction, in such surroundings and company she became a social butterfly, almost overnight.

This existence did not last long; her parents were seeking to make the most advantageous marriage possible, with money the key factor. Several eligible suitors were rejected out-of-hand before her ambitious parents arranged for her to be married to thirty-eight year old Monsieur Jacques Guyon: a successful and wealthy businessman with the right connections to a distinguished French family. Arranged marriages were very much the order of the day and poor Jeanne Marie signed the marriage document without fully realising what she was doing. Not that it would have made any difference. Everyone agreed that it was a good marriage; Jacques Guyon was very rich and moved in the right circles; what else mattered? Jeanne Marie's romantic hopes before the marriage were soon shattered once the society wedding was over. He husband was not only ugly but suffered from gout which frequently laid him up in bed for months at a time. Worst of all he did not love her. Jeanne Marie had not even met her husband until three days before the wedding, but at the age of not quite sixteen her fate was sealed.

At her new family home, the young Madame Jeanne Marie Guyon soon found that she was not going to be allowed to be the mistress in her own house. Her widowed and wizened mother-in-law was a tyrant who dominated her son and the whole miserable household. Although they were very rich she was miserly and from the first set out to ensure that her young daughter-in-law was put firmly in place. The sad and disillusioned young girl never had a chance. She was no match for this cruel old woman, who, not content with dominating the young bride, also deliberately encouraged the servants to be insolent and rude and to make life unbearable for their new mistress.

The cruel pressure eased for a little time when Jeanne Marie became pregnant and, after about twelve months of married life, produced her first son, Armand. She was very ill just before the birth and her life was feared for but she survived and the birth of a son and heir to the Guyon family fortune was greeted with great joy. Her baby was a comfort to her and she needed every crumb of that rare commodity to endure her fate. A reversal in the family fortunes was blamed on the young Madame Guyon, as was just about everything else which went wrong in the Guyon household.

The news of the early death of Jeanne's devoted nun-stepsister was another terrible blow. All these circumstances conspired to drive her to seek consolation in religion. She simplified her dress, recommenced reading devotional books, and mingled her prayers with many penances. Little by little, with help from various people along the way, the light of salvation began to dawn upon her. During a visit to her family she met a deeply religious lady, who, though suffering exile from her country, was clearly in possession of God's peace in her heart. She discerned that although young Madame Guyon was doing many religious duties there was a lack of understanding of the simplicity of true prayer. Madame Guyon wanted so much what this woman had but still could not find it. The homecoming of her cousin after four years of service in China, also helped; Monsieur de Toissi was one to whom she felt free to open her heart. She did not find what she was seeking but she saw something in his life which encouraged her to continue with her quest.

Madame Guyon was carrying her second child when news came that her father was very ill and she hurried home as quickly as possible. Through undertaking such a journey in her condition she was taken ill herself. Nevertheless, the visit proved to be providential. Her father introduced her to a devout Franciscan monk who had just visited him in his sickness and made a profound impression upon him. This monk had but recently spent five years in solitude seeking the face of God. He emerged with a heart burning with love for God and the souls of men and felt that God had definitely led him to that area with a promise that he would be used to lead an influential person to the Saviour. Madame Guyon poured out her heart to this true man of God. She told him of her hunger to know God, of her seeking Him by Bible reading, attending church, penances, and charitable deeds, but all to no avail. He told her that she had been unsuccessful because she had sought externally what can only be found in the soul, and advised her to seek God in her heart and she would not fail to find Him. Those simple words spoken in the power of God's Spirit went right to her heart and soon, though she could not explain how it had happened, she was gloriously changed. She knew that God's presence had entered her life. She was too happy to sleep that night. So it was that at twenty years of age on July 22nd, 1668 Madame Guyon at last experienced the joy of salvation in Christ. She yielded herself fully and wholly to the Lord from that moment. She withdrew from all the pleasures of high society. Prayer was no longer a duty but a joy and pleasure; hours on her knees passed like minutes, and the Lord Jesus Christ filled her vision.

The change in Jeanne Marie's life was dramatic. She set out to rescue some of the young women who had been sucked into prositution through their involvement with the increasingly permissive society under young King Louis. She succeeded not only in rehabilitating some of them but in leading them to her new-found Saviour and Lord. In addition she visited the sick, cared for the poor, and gave instruction where needed. Her conversion and changed lifestyle aroused criticism and opposition in society and she became the butt of many jibes, but nothing could now move her from her course.

Madame Guyon renewed efforts to win the favour and affection of her husband and even of her vindictive mother-in-law. Late in 1668 she bore a second son, with a daughter the following year. For two years she was full of joy and peace in spite of the fact that life was still very difficult for her in the Guyon household. Then in 1670 her faith was severely tested. Her children were taken ill with the dreaded smallpox, which she herself eventually contracted. She became desperately ill and lay at death's door for a time. Although she recovered she was marked for life by the pock scars; she accepted the loss of her beauty as part of the price God was asking her to pay, but less harder to bear was the death of their precious two-year-old younger son with smallpox. It was a good thing for her that she found a new friend and spiritual adviser and confidant soon after this in the person of Father Francois La Combe. He became a longstanding and loyal friend who stood with her in many trials. Her husband tolerated his wife's charity work but deeply resented her preoccupation with the Bible and her obsession with prayer and church attendance. On the fourth anniversary of her conversion at the suggestion of another dear friend, Sister Genevieve Granger, she dedicated herself afresh to Christ in the same form of spiritual marriage to Christ that is taken by nuns. She signed the document as seriously as she had signed her marriage vows on her wedding day but with a great deal more love and devotion.

Over the next few years Jeanne Marie suffered several more successive blows which tested her devotion to the utmost. She awakened suddenly at 4.00 am on a summer morning in 1672 with the premonition of her father's death. That same afternoon a messenger hurried to fetch her with the news that her father was dangerously ill. She immediately set off to him on what was a long and dangerous journey of some eighty miles, travelling through the night and all the next day, but she arrived to find that he was not only dead, but (because of the excessive heat) had already been buried. Jeanne's mother had died some time before this but she had been much closer to her father and she greatly felt his loss. Not many days afterwards her three-year-old daughter suffered a brain haemorrhage and died in bed. She had been a beautiful child and Madame Guyon was closely attached to her, but with great fortitude she submitted herself wholly to the Lord in this trial of her faith.

Madam Guyon was now left with one son and when he fell ill and remained in a desperate condition for a time, her faith was tested to the utmost. However, her friend Sister Granger arrived and prayed for the little boy and he was wonderfully healed and his life spared. But Jeanne Marie was quite devastated when a few months later this good spiritual woman, who had been such a friend to her, passed away. With her husband's permission she then decided to go to a convent called St Cyr's for a spiritual retreat. This was a strict order of nuns which practised self-inflicted physical pain by instruments as penances which brought the soul nearer to God. In her desperate condition Jeanne Marie resorted once again to these measures. She fasted taking only a little fruitjuice for several days. She scourged herself with knotted cords until her body was covered in blood, and even strapped on her bare flesh a belt of horsehair and nettles along with a girdle full of sharp nails. In addition she put on elbow and knee bracelets studded with chunks of metal. She tortured herself unmercifully but she found that it was all in vain, and left the convent disappointed but wiser, realising fully that such self-discipline was of no value whatsoever. It was a painful way to learn but it cured her of this terrible tradition and enabled her to speak with authority and conviction to those similarly deluded.

Throughout these years Madame Guyon was a faithful and dutiful wife to her selfish husband. In all she bore him three sons and two daughters, losing one son with smallpox, and one daughter with a brain haemorrhage. In 1676 when her husband was dying she hardly left his bedside for twenty-four days and before he died he begged her forgiveness for the shameful way he had treated her throughout their marriage.

Jacques Guyon died on July 21st, 1676 leaving her a young widow of twenty-eight years, with two boys of eleven and three, and a baby girl of just a few weeks. Madame Guyon soon surprised everyone with her efficient handling of the estate after his death and she made no secret that it was due to prayer. The friction continued with her cantankerous old mother-in-law and six months after the death of her husband the young widow moved from the family mansion into a house of her own, with her three children. Financially she was well provided for and she was able to devote herself to much prayer and study of the Bible and religious books. Many of the Catholic devotional classics she was interested in were in Latin and so she set herself the difficult task of learning that language. Her one desire was to find the will of God for her life.

After some four years she found that during her times of prayer the place Geneva was constantly repeated as by an inner voice. As a good Catholic she was appalled at the very mention of this city which was the centre of Calvin's Protestantism. She wrote to her friend Father La Combe at Thonon and asked him to set aside July 22nd, 1680, (the twelfth anniversary of her conversion) as a day of prayer and fasting when they would both seek God's guidance for her life. Following this day she realized with joy that henceforth she was to regard herself as 'married to Christ' in the sense of being entirely devoted to Him. She would have loved to have entered a nunnery but felt that this would be unfair on her children and cut her off from them completely. Nevertheless she was eventually forced to face the fact that to obey the call of God in her life she was going to have to leave her precious sons to be cared for and educated by others. It was a hard decision but once made she was eager to be on the move.

After consulting with a friend, Jeanne Marie decided to head for Gex, a small town near the southernmost tip of Burgundy, about a dozen miles from Geneva; but first she must obtain the permission of the bishop of that region. Learning that this was Bishop D'Aranthon and that he was in Paris on a visit she arranged to see him and tell him of her plans. These included the possibility of building a hospital or convent with some of her considerable inherited wealth. The good bishop was delighted at the prospect of a devout, rich aristocrat like Madame Guyon, aiding the poor in his region. He did, however, caution her to be careful to moderate her religious zeal which was beginning to upset quite a few in the church, including her stepbrother, Father La Mothe, who had become an influential priest in the capital city and at court. Father La Mothe had the ear of King Louis XIV and was ambitious and greedy and had designs upon Madame Guyon's property. The stepbrother who had plagued the life out of his little sister in their childhood was destined to torment her cruelly during this new phase of her life. He deeply resented her meddling as a lay-person in the affairs of the church which to him were the province of priesthood. It was not unknown for people who made trouble to be seized and removed to the Bastille secretly and without trial.

Madame Guyon sensed that she was in danger and arranged to leave Paris under cover of night by boat down the River Seine, with her five-year-old daughter, two maidservants, and a friend called Sister Garnier. The long journey by river and road took around two weeks and they arrived at the residence of Bishop D'Aranthon at Annecy on July 21st, 1681. With the Bishop's blessing she then travelled on to Gex, situated at the foot of Mount St Claude in the Jura Mountains, only a few miles from Geneva. She took up temporary accommodation with some Sisters of Charity and rejoiced at her safe arrival. She had a sense of destiny in being in Gex and spent long hours in prayer. Many times she woke in the middle of the night with such a sense of God's presence that she could not go back to sleep but rose to enjoy glorious times of praise and close communion with the Lord. Spiritual enlightenment and enrichment of soul resulted from these times of seeking God.

There was a great deal of poverty and sickness in the town and she busied herself in the practical ministry of feeding the poor and nursing the sick. Although she was happy and content in this work she could not escape the feeling that this was still not the great work to which God was calling her. She shared her perplexity with Father La Combe who advised her to set aside time to pray to find the perfect will of God for her life. Part of the answer came in a revelation from God that sanctification as well as salvation was by faith. This was the very opposite of all that she had been taught, but she knew from her own bitter experiences that ceremonial observances and cruel penances did nothing for the soul in its quest for true holiness. She knew that this was the message she had to share and commenced to do so. Meanwhile, Madame Guyon's stepbrother, Father La Mothe, was incensed when he discovered that she had escaped from Paris and plotted to bring her back. On discovering her whereabouts he tried to entice her to return by writing a deceitful letter about her mother-in-law being dangerously ill, but again his plan failed.

The primitive conditions in the area where Madame Guyon was now living and working soon proved too much for her. The long, hot summer, contaminated water, and poor food, combined to undermine her health quite seriously and the Sisters of Charity in the convent where she lived wrote pleading with Father La Combe to come immediately. On receiving the letter this good man walked through the night to reach her as soon as possible. On arrival he laid his hands upon Jeanne Marie's fever-burning forehead and prayed fervently for her deliverance. Almost immediately her temperature dropped and she was miraculously healed in such a way that it impressed all who knew the circumstances. The news of the miracle quickly spread around the area. But the greater miracle lay in the increased spiritual wisdom and understanding which God had given her by His Spirit through this experience. She had a clear perception of the doctrine of salvation and sanctification by faith in Christ, and was now able to communicate this effectively to others. Hers became a ministry of counselling individuals or small groups rather than preaching.

Madame Guyon had now outstripped her mentor, Father La Combe, and it was she who patiently instructed him until at last he was able to turn from all his self-efforts and religious endeavours to make himself holy, and to trust only the atoning work of Christ and the Word of God.

One day, a spiritual recluse who lived in a continual state of prayer, spoke to Madame Guyon with prophetic insight and power, assuring her that she was destined by God to be used to help many find Christ, but warning her that it would not be fulfilled without having to suffer and bear many crosses. This was exactly what happened: many received her words but opposition began to mount and from some in high places in the Catholic church. Her teaching sounded too much like that of Martin Luther and Protestantism.

Bishop D'Aranthon, an early ally, now began to get worried by the mounting opposition to Madame Guyon, but she was doing such a great work amongst the poor that he tolerated her. Furthermore, he had high hopes of persuading her to erect a religious establishment in Gex which would have added to his prestige. When she obstinately refused he turned against her and Father La Combe. He began to denounce and threaten them, and set out to trap Father La Combe by inviting him to preach and then drawing up a list of errors in the sermon he had preached and sending them to Rome in order that they might find him guilty of heresy! To the Bishop's annoyance Rome never replied to his epistle. The Bishop now began to vent his wrath on Madame Guyon. He made one last desperate effort to get his hands on her wealth by offering to make her a prioress of a religious order if she would finance it. On her rejecting his proposal he banished her from his diocese.

Madame Guyon had no alternative but to leave and chose to visit her little daughter (now aged six) at the Ursuline Convent in Thonon, Savoy. During this visit her daughter went down with smallpox but in answer to the prayers of Father La Combe she made a rapid recovery. With Father La Combe's permission Madame Guyon was able to stay for a spiritual retreat at Thonon. As she gave herself to fasting and prayer she received a strong impression that God wanted her to start writing, and this was the start of a tremendous ministry. She became a prolific writer. Through her books she soon became famous throughout Europe and many were blessed and helped to find rest and peace in Christ. It was an amazing ministry which developed beyond her wildest imaginings. At Thonon she experienced a number of visions and received revelations and prophecies. People now began to seek her out, and in the power of the Spirit with a new simplicity of faith Madame Guyon sought to lead them to rest upon God alone through Christ. She pointed sinners directly to Christ, faithfully exposing the sinfulness of the human heart, the uselessness of good works to merit salvation, and the impossibility of acceptance by God, except through the application of the atoning blood of Christ, received through faith. Many were born again through her personal work and soon a revival broke out in Thonon which spread across the Lake to Lausanne.

Madame Guyon was now experiencing the power of God's Spirit in her life. She manifested an amazing insight into the problems of people she counselled. Her faith was rising all the time. When one of her maidservants was ill she commanded her to get up in the name of Jesus, as she was healed. The girl obeyed and rose perfectly healed, from what some had imagined could well prove to be a fatal sickness. Madame Guyon experienced such happenings on many occasions, and made it known that if people received the Word and acted on it they were healed, but if they doubted and made excuses like saying they would be healed in God's time, invariably nothing happened and she was conscious that the healing power returned to bless her, instead of bringing relief to the sufferer.

The whole town of Thonon was stirred and many people sought and found God. There was a special revival among the young girls who had to work long hours for little money, and they prayed as they worked. They formed themselves into little neighbourhood groups to help and encourage each other in the faith, but opposition mounted and the church broke up these small gatherings.

Wherever she went Madame Guyon now found herself with a large following and her days were often filled with people seeking counselling from 6.00 am to 8.00 pm. In 1683 she wrote *Spiritual Torrents*, a book which was virtually her testimony, and destined to become a famous best-seller for generations to come. She remained for two fruitful years at Thonon but through mounting persecution and ill-health she moved to Turin. There she was wonderfully used to bring about the conversion and blessing of two or three leading priests, all of whom had at first bitterly opposed her. As well as writing many books and tracts she was a profuse letter-writer, faithfully following up many people she had led to Christ and giving them sound spiritual instruction.

From Turin she came back into France and in 1684 settled in Grenoble. Her fame had preceded her and soon she was busy from morning till night dealing with people who wanted spiritual counsel. Many were born again and experienced an immediate and dramatic conversion, including the head of a religious house, who after initial opposition to Madame Guyon was led by her to a saving trust in God and left her presence 'a new man in Christ'.

She wrote another book, *A Short Method of Prayer*, which God used to help a great many monks, priests and nuns, who had been seeking vainly to find peace with Him through ceremony and penances.

However, the Word of God was always Madame Guyon's great delight and at Grenoble she commenced writing a series of commentaries which ultimately covered the Old and New Testaments. She read the Scriptures in Latin and French, and, praying for the anointing and help of the Holy Spirit, she wrote her commentaries which became a blessing to countless thousands. Much of her writing was done at night. When finished there were twenty volumes, twelve on the Old and eight on the New Testament. Her commentary on the Song of Solomon in which she expounded her teaching on the union of the soul with Christ was destined to become a spiritual classic for centuries to come.

During Madame Guyon's stay at Grenoble a revival broke out in the spring and summer which touched all classes. She led a knight to Christ. Also a poor nun, who had been insane for eight years, was instantly delivered through her prayers and made whole. However, due to increasing pressures against her she finally had to leave Grenoble in 1686. She then went to Marseilles but her presence caused an immediate uproar and she remained only eight days. Some went to the bishop and asked him to banish her immediately and destroy her book on prayer, but when he read it he liked it and when he met Madame Guyon was most favourably impressed. Although her stay was a brief one there was lasting fruit from it.

Jeanne Marie Guyon returned to Paris that same year after an absence of five years; now thirty-nine years old, she was spiritually mature and able to converse effectively with people of the highest intellect. A house was hired in the city and she had the immense joy and pleasure of collecting her little family of two sons and a daughter round her once more. Her social standing gave her links with the higher classes and with great courage she openly shared her faith in Christ with many of them. But as soon as her stepbrother, Father La Mothe, learned tht she was in the city he plotted against her, and against Father La Combe. In little more than a year Father La Combe was arrested and shut up in the Bastille. He was moved around to Lourde, then Vincennes, and to Oleron. He was cruelly incarcerated in vile conditions for twenty-seven years and died insane through his ill-treatment.

Madame Guyon openly advocated praying directly to God, by-passing Mary and the saints as unnecessary and she also let it be known that she was against the sale of masses; all of which was guaranteed to raise a storm of bitter opposition. When King Louis XIV revoked the Edict of Nantes in 1685 (which had given protection to French Protestants) with a view to gaining the favour of the Pope, the situation became dangerous for Madame Guyon, even though she always maintained that she was a true Roman Catholic. Through the cunning and deceit of her stepbrother, Father La Mothe, it was not long before charges were brought against her. The Archbishop of Paris condemned Madame Guyon for heresy. It was her teaching that justification came by faith in

Jesus Christ alone, and sanctification likewise, which the church hated—coupled with her refusal to worship the saints or Mary.

She was arrested on January 29th, 1688 and detained on the King's order at the Convent of Visitation of Mary at Antoine in the suburbs of the city. Her health was low due to the severe winter and she found it hard to have to part from her twelve-year old daughter; but in spite of the adverse circumstances she enjoyed the presence of God and rejoiced before Him. She commenced writing her autobiography and filled her solitary hours with prayer and Bible reading as well as letter writing. An opportunity to gain an early freedom came when the king wrote offering her a pardon if she would agree to the marriage of her daughter with the Marquis of Chanvolon, but she bravely refused. Several times, over a period of eight months, Madame Guyon was interrogated; every effort was made to trap her, including the use of a forged letter, but she regained her freedom in October 1688, largely due to the intervention of some of her lady friends in high places, with whom she had faithfully shared her faith.

Madame Guyon was used by God to influence some of the key figures of France, the most notable being Father Fenelon, who was generally acknowledged as the intellectual giant of his times. He was appointed by King Louis as personal tutor to the heir apparent to the throne, and under his godly influence this boy showed signs of a change for the better. Fenelon was much at the palace and in 1697 he was appointed Archbishop of Cambray. He met with Madame Guyon and through her influence was won over to much of her teaching. When the opposition against her increased he championed her cause but her enemies would not be denied. They plotted and schemed until she was charged with heresy. Although the investigation against her was inconclusive, her implacable opponent Bishop Bossuet succeeded in March 1695 in getting the commission completed which found that thirty of her propositions leaned towards Protestantism and that her writings bordered on heresy and were unacceptable to the church. He did not rest until Madame Guyon was arrested along with her faithful maid, and imprisoned in the Castle Vincennes on the 31st December 1695. She passed her time singing songs of praise, many of which were her own composition. Nothing could quench her joy in Christ. In August 1696 she was transferred to Vaugirard Prison, where the conditions were better. She continued with her writing, but outside her enemies were still not content. In September 1698 they finally succeeded in getting her transferred to the dreaded Bastille. At fifty years of age it was a terrible ordeal. The walls were twelve to eighteen feet thick, which meant that prisoners could not see the ground or the sky from the one small window which was open all the year round. The prisoners were known only by numbers so that their identity was concealed from the guards. All possessions were removed from all prisoners without exception, and they were allowed only a Bible, a comb, prayer-book and rosary.

Madame Guyon endured this solitary confinement for four years. A confession would have secured her release immediately but such was unthinkable to her. In 1702 her sentence was re-viewed and partly because of her ill-health she was released. She emerged pale, thin and grey and looking older than her fifty-four years.

In spite of her poor health she lived until June 9th, 1717. She died at the age of sixty-nine and was buried in the Church of the Cordeliers at Blois, France. In her last will and testament she said, 'Within Thy hands, O God, I leave my soul, not relying for my salvation on any good that is in me, but solely on Thy mercies and the merits and sufferings of my Lord Jesus Christ.'

Her writings lived on after her death to influence the Moravians, the Quakers, and the Methodists. John Wesley and Count Zinzendorf praised her writings, as did Judson and Watchman Nee in more recent times. Three hundred years after her imprisonment in the Bastille, she remains an inspiration to all who seek to know Christ in a deeper way and to engage in spiritual warfare.

6: Praying Hyde

In the spring of 1911 a united mission was in progress in the English town of Shrewsbury but it looked like being a gigantic flop. The churches had invited the well-known American evangelistic duo, Chapman and Alexander, but the initial response was poor and the necessary enthusiasm missing. The evangelist, Wilbur Chapman, was clearly disappointed at the small numbers who supported the beginning of the mission and called the ministers together to see what could be done to remedy the situation. Charles Alexander, his song-leader and a man of prayer, was equally dispirited and the meeting with the ministers did nothing to raise their hopes. It seemed to be accepted that such missions in Shrewsbury 'never went over the top', and nothing that Wilbur Chapman said in his pointed address to them could rouse them from their apathy. In the end the evangelist was so disappointed that he left the meeting early. The mission continued with low attendances and almost no results. Then Wilbur Chapman received a letter from a Welsh missionary, Rev Pengwern Jones, who was home on furlough from India. In it he told the evangelist that a missionary friend was coming to Shrewsbury especially to pray with them for the mission's success. Would Mr Chapman find another praying person to intercede along with this special friend? This the evangelist was more than glad to do and he appointed Mr Davis of the Pocket Testament League.

Almost immediately the Rev Jones' 'missionary friend' arrived and the tide turned. Suddenly the hall from being thinly attended was packed and when the invitation was given some fifty men responded.

Dr Wilbur Chapman was a godly and spiritually sensitive person and that night as he was leaving the hall he asked the 'mysterious intercessor' to pray for *him*. The man came to Chapman's room, locked the door, and then dropped to his knees—the evangelist joined him. Five minutes of silence followed—but Chapman found his heart beating faster than usual in expectation. There was an atmosphere in that room and the evangelist found himself weeping. God was there. As he waited his visitor uttered his first words, 'Oh God . . . .' Through his own tears Wilbur Chapman could see the tears also streaming down the thin, pinched face of his visitor. Another long period of silence followed, then Chapman felt his visitor's arm around his shoulder as the man began to pray. Such petitions then rose from the heart of this intercessor the like of which Chapman had never before experienced. He knew this man was touching the throne of Almighty God. When he finally rose from his knees Wilbur Chapman knew what real prayer was. His mysterious intercessor stayed in Shrewsbury for a whole week and the mission was transformed. Churches were revived, the apathetic ministers were stirred and blessed, many were brought to Christ, and Chapman and Alexander knew that the prayers of one man had made the difference. Chapman told the story again and again of his encounter with the man who is still better known by his nickname of 'Praying' Hyde, than by his Christian name of John Hyde. When this incident occurred Hyde was a dying man, returning home to America via England after nineteen years of missionary service in Northern India.

John Hyde was born in 1865 at Carthage, Illinois, America. His father, Rev Smith Harris Hyde, DD., was a Presbyterian minister, with Mrs Hyde a worthy help to him and a wonderful mother to their three sons and three daughters. Mrs Hyde loved music and possessed a fine singing voice, and the memory of these talents always lived with John, along with the Christian teaching and training she instilled in him throughout his childhood. John's father was a faithful pastor to his people and John's ambition was to follow in his father's footsteps in the ministry. With this in mind he followed his older brother, Edmund, to the M'Cormick Seminary. For the first two years there John was 'just one of the crowd'; he was quite a good student but being a somewhat quiet person and rather hard of hearing, he tended to simply merge into the college scene. Until, that is, in his third year when he was devastated by the sudden death of his brother Edmund—who had been preparing to go to the mission field.

When that happened the challenge of taking his brother's place suddenly loomed large before John, but he struggled against it; his personal preference was very much with the home field. Many of his fellow classmates were preparing themselves for overseas service but it took the jolt of his brother's death to change John's mind. After a long struggle he made the great surrender and told the Lord that he was willing to go wherever He desired. From that moment the issue was settled and he quickly became the leading advocate in the college for missionary service. Prayer became a new power in his life and the other students began to sit up and take notice. Very soon he was the means of persuading others to join him in volunteering for overseas missions. He was ambitious to become a great missionary and he applied himself with new keenness to his studies, resulting in a good BA degree of which he was not a little proud.

Having settled that his future service lay in India John determined to master the Indian languages. By the time that he was due to sail to India in 1892 he had grown in confidence and self-assurance. When he boarded the steamer in New York to sail to India he found a letter awaiting him from a very dear ministerial colleague and friend of his father's. This man had wanted to become a missionary but had been prevented from doing so. He was greatly interested in John and delighted that he was going to India; John also had a great affection and respect for this good man. John recognised the handwriting and opened it gladly but when he read it he was so angry that he screwed it up into a ball and threw it in the corner of his cabin. Fuming with indignation at what he had read he slammed the cabin door behind him and went up on deck to cool off. The letter was only a short one but the words which had offended young John were to the effect that the minister would not cease praying for John until John was filled with the Holy Spirit! The very idea of suggesting that he, John Hyde, BA., was not filled with the Spirit—wasn't he going out to India?—wasn't he determined to excel as a missionary?—wasn't the implication of the letter that he was not fitted and equipped for the task after all his years at college? But as he paced the deck he felt distinctly uncomfortable. John knew the writer of the letter to be a true man of God who lived close to his Lord. Deep down in his heart he knew that the letter was right—he really was not fit to be a missionary. In a very different frame of mind he returned to his cabin to rescue the crumpled letter and to read it again and again. He still felt annoyed but the conviction grew that the man was right and he was wrong. The inward battle continued over the next two or three days but finally John capitulated and despairingly asked the Lord to fill him with the Holy Spirit. His relief was immediate but with this also came the revelation of his own selfish ambitions. Throughout the long voyage he continued to pray for the Spirit and determined that whatever the cost he would not rest until he was truly filled with the Holy Spirit.

John spent his first days in India with a missionary of wide experience called Dr Newton, and one day accompanied him to an open-air service. John had to have the message interpreted to him as he had not yet learnt the language. The interpreter explained that the message was about Jesus being the real Saviour from sin. Afterwards a well-educated Indian who had been listening approached the missionary and asked him whether he himself had been saved in that way. The question went home to John's heart for he knew that there was one besetting sin in his life which still plagued him. He returned to his room to shut himself in with the Lord in prayer and there he earnestly sought his Saviour for deliverance from this sin. He faced up to the issue that this matter must be settled or he would have to return to American to take up some other work. As he waited in prayer he received the assurance in his heart that the Lord was able to deliver him from all sin and that He had a definite work for him to do in India. The matter was settled there and then and he was able to testify to the victory which Christ had given him and to His abiding faithfulness.

John Hyde's sphere of service lay in North-West India in the Punjab, which in those days before the secession was wholly in India. The population was a mixed one of Muslims, Sikhs and Hindus, with the Muslims predominant. It was a difficult area and it was generally acknowledged that it was much harder for missionary work in the North of India than in the South. In John's area at one time there were just three women missionaries, himself and another man, among almost one million non-Christians.

In spite of the vital life-changing experiences which he had passed through since leaving home, John's first few years as a missionary were not especially distinguished by any great happenings. He tended to be slow in his speaking, and his partial deafness was a definite drawback, especially in acquiring the languages he needed to master, Urdu and Punjabi. Indeed at one time he actually sent in his resignation to the Synod in despair at mastering the language owing to his deafness. But with it came another letter from the people of his village begging the Synod not to accept the resignation because 'although he never speaks the language of our lips, he speaks the language of our hearts'.

The Bible was becoming increasingly precious to John during this time, so much so that he began to neglect his language studies in favour of mastering the Word of God. This brought him a rebuke from the mission authorities but in the end he became an easy speaker in Urdu and Punjabi as well as a gifted expositor of the Scriptures. Nevertheless, John still had his problems in these early years. The other missionaries found him something of an enigma; he seemed to lack the zeal and enthusiasm expected of a young missionary. To many he seemed morose and shy, although when people did get to know him better they found that he had a very real sense of humour. He appeared to be something of a visionary. When people spoke to him, many times he gave the impression that he had not heard them—and perhaps he had not because of his deafness. At other times they found that he had heard them but he took an inordinately long time to reply. It was all rather disturbing especially when he turned his bright blue eyes on people and seemed to look right through them. He found the climate and conditions a strain and once he wrote, 'India is so exhausting and I do not want to stay here'. In spite of everything he stuck it out and those early years were not entirely without fruit. The friendship of one of the senior missionaries, a Rev Ullman, who had been in India for fifty-five years, and under whom John was placed for a time for language study and other instruction, was a special blessing to him. He entered into a new appreciation of the power of the precious blood of Christ after months of special seeking for sanctification. Sent out into the surrounding villages with Indian preachers, although he was still only able to take a very minor part because of his slowness in mastering the language, he rejoiced to see God working in the salvation of men and women. In one village they had the joy of baptising eight low-caste people.

Slowly but surely John Hyde progressed in those early years until he was able to preach and converse acceptably in the native languages, and spiritually he increased in power as he gave himself to prayer and study of the Word. In 1895 he worked with another missionary in Lahore and Ferozepore, and they were encouraged as they experienced what was something of a little revival for two or three weeks. John was conscious of the anointing of the Spirit upon him as he gave the Word to these simple people in such a way that he himself was amazed how clearly he was able to communicate the truth to them. At their early morning prayer meetings they had the joy of seeing new converts learning to pray with them. Prayer was needed because persecution came to these converts—and the missionaries—especially from the high-caste people. Some of the new Christians were actually physically beaten and the missionaries themselves were threatened. All of this drove John to more prayer and in this way he came to a new and deeper understanding of God. The Lord was shaping this special vessel for greater things but the work would take several more quite painful years.

The year 1896 was disappointing for John in that there were no conversions in the villages; after the encouragement they had received the previous year it was perplexing to him—and he (along with other missionaries) gave himself to special prayer to find the reason. Things improved the following year and he greatly enjoyed a long break of six weeks in Poona, which he spent in the home of another missionary (Mr R. P. Wilder) whose balanced and happy Christianity was deeply appreciated by John. He was encouraged to find that the converts were taking a greater interest in the work than ever before.

In 1898 John was suddenly laid low with typhoid fever. His recovery was slow and long taking seven months. During this period he gave himself afresh to prayer and his prayer was constantly that of Jabez, 'Enlarge my border,' (1 Chronicles 4:10). The mission was under financial pressure making life more difficult for all the missionaries, but they responded by unitedly praying every Sunday for God to pour out His Spirit upon them. On returning to his station at Ferozepore, though still very weak, John was able to do itinerary work and rejoiced to find a new responsiveness resulting in many turning to Christ. These he duly baptised and ensured that they were given teaching in Christian basics.

In 1899 John took the important step of beginning to spend whole nights in prayer. Throughout the winter he had given himself more than ever before to the burden of interceding for others. The results of the missionaries' work throughout that year had been scanty with just a few inquirers and a small number of baptisms and this was a factor in driving him to more prayer. Needless to say the more time he spent in prayer the less John's fellow missionaries understood him. To some he seemed in great danger of becoming 'fanatical' and dangerously extreme. Hyde had, however, already faced this in prayer with God and he was ready for opposition, willing to be called crazy, prepared to take up his cross. One missionary lectured him about his lack of wisdom and his crazy notions and his unwillingness to be guided by his seniors. It was fortunate for John that throughout his first seven years in India he was privileged to live in the home of a wise and saintly missionary, Dr Newton, something which he was not slow to appreciate.

The two years 1900 and 1901 were years of definite progress in spite of growing misunderstanding by some. Hyde rejoiced to see very definite answers to prayer and increasing evidence of the Holy Spirit's working in the local church. When he wrote home he shared his faith that the new century would be a time of Pentecostal power and even a double portion of the Pentecostal Spirit. How right he proved to be! He envisaged this as a mighty outpouring of God's Spirit resulting in deep conviction and great multitudes turning to Christ. He saw the nineteenth century as good but not up to the level of the apostolic age, but believed that the twentieth century was destined to be one in which the full life of apostolic Christianity would be restored to the church. His prayer was for a church holy in life, triumphant in faith, self-sacrificing in service, with one aim, to preach Christ crucified to the uttermost part of the earth.

Hyde had his first furlough in 1902 and it was a great joy for him to find the church in America showing every evidence of new spiritual life and blessing. He believed that the full realisation of revival at home and in India lay in receiving what the Scriptures taught about the fulness of the Spirit. The message he shared whenever he had the opportunity was: 'You shall receive power after that the Holy Ghost is come upon' (Acts 1:8). He had come a long way since the day, ten years before, when he crumpled up in anger the letter which told him of his need to be filled with the Spirit.

John's return to India in 1903 was still not easy, and he experienced not a few twinges of homesickness as he faced once again the heat and dust and drudgery of missionary life in North-West India. But God was beginning to touch other hearts as well as his own about the need for intercession and around April, 1904, John and some of his friends formed the Punjab Prayer Union, the burden of which was to pray for revival. Among the other American Presbyterian missionaries were John's friends, E.P. Newton and E.M. Wherry. Their aims were to pray for special blessing on the newly-organised Conventions at Sialkot, for a spirit of unity, for guidance and wisdom, and for revival in India. Members were asked to set aside half an hour each day as soon after noon as possible to pray for this awakening and to be willing and committed to pray until revival came.

The convention at Sialkot in the summer was organised for the deepening of the spiritual life of the workers and missionaries; it was to be a place for Bible study and prayer. John was again very much involved in planning this along with two other men of prayer, R.M. Cheyne Paterson and George Turner. They all felt that the life of the church in the Punjab was far below the biblical standard and this was the principal reason why so few souls were coming to Christ.

Hyde and his friend Paterson met together one month before the first Convention to pray for a mighty outpouring of God's Spirit. Nine days later they were joined by George Turner, and the three of them continued to wait before God, night and day, with fasting, crying, pleading, agonising over the church in India and for the millions of lost souls around them. The three of them were of one mind, one heart and in one accord. For thirty days, this vigil of intercession was maintained. The price was tremendous but they willingly paid it. This Convention marked the great turning point in Hyde's spiritual progress. He emerged from his wrestling with God, transformed—as did Jacob at Peniel. Hyde was now a prince spiritually, having power with God and with men.

It seems that around three hundred gathered at that first Convention; not a great number, but it was the dawn of a new day. Hyde's Bible studies during this Convention were of a very high order and affected all who heard them. One evening he addressed a special meeting for men only, whilst the women were having their own gathering in another place. It transpired that Hyde had prayed all night and fasted all day. He revealed that he had been in conflict with God over whether he should share with them some of the intimate things God had done in his inner life in giving him victory over various sins. He did not want to share them, but he felt that God was clearly telling him that he must do so. Finally he submitted to God and opened his heart to the gathered group of men. He did not speak for very long, perhaps around twenty minutes, and then he asked them to pray. Soon one after another was confessing his sins and crying to God for forgiveness and mercy. Lives were lastingly changed that night and the way opened for the coming revival. 1904 saw the beginning of a series of outpourings of God's Spirit in North-West India. News of the revival which had broken out in Wales that same year eventually reached India and served to fan the flames and increase the praying and faith of Hyde and his friends, as well as a multitude of others right across India.

Prayer was now the grand obsession of Hyde's life; more and more he gave himself to prayer. Some did not understand this and were open and sometimes even bitter in their criticism of him, but Hyde never showed any bitterness in return. He was not, however, a hermit, or a recluse; he had a great burden for precious souls and was willing to go to any lengths to win people for Christ. He would travel past his stop on the train if he was engaged in vital soul-winning activity with a fellow passenger! (Although this too, brought adverse reaction from some of his colleagues, especially if he was late for an appointment as a consequence.)

In the spring of 1905 the Punjab Prayer Union met again and the leaders together with Hyde gave themselves to some ten days of united prayer before the Annual Meeting. They were days of fasting and all-night watching which were a preparation for the second Sialkot Convention later in the year. At Sialkot John Hyde literally lived in the prayer room— day and night he was there. The words which burned in his heart and sustained him in this amazing vigil of almost unremitting prayer were, 'I have set watchmen upon thy walls, O Jerusalem, which shall never hold their peace day or night: ye that are the Lord's remembrancers, take ye no rest and give Him no rest till He establish, and till He make Jerusalem a praise in the earth' (Isaiah 62:6, 7). Hyde and some of the other leaders had come into an intimacy with God where His will was supreme. They were on holy ground. The results were seen when Hyde shared the morning Bible readings; his messages were extremely searching. One morning he asked his fellow workers: 'Is the Holy Spirit first in your pulpits?' as he ministered to them from John 15:26, 27 'He (the Holy Spirit, the Comforter) shall bear witness of Me, and ye also shall bear witness of Me.' Many were broken as a result of that message but with the brokenness came renewal and joy. Hyde himself had his own confession to make. He shared with the group that God had told him to do something, and he had done it—but unwillingly. He returned to the prayer room weeping and confessing this and asking them to pray for him that he might do it joyfully. The prayer was answered and a little later he re-entered the room with great joy and spoke just three words: 'O Heavenly Father . . .' What followed was apparently akin to a repeat of the day of

Pentecost in Acts 2, when the Spirit came like a rushing mighty wind upon the assembled disciples. All present bowed before the wind of God's Spirit. Confessions of sins were made with tears but soon they turned to shouts of joy and victory, and like those in that upper room in Jerusalem, they too were filled with new wine.

The Spirit of prayer came upon those gathered and all responded in their own way: some knelt, some prostrated themselves on their faces before Almighty God, some praised, some sat. There was glorious freedom, an absence of criticism, and a sense of God's Holy presence day and night. Some were supernaturally sustained to go without sleep and watched in prayer night after night. As a result of that Convention the revival spread throughout the region. Mission schools and colleges in the area experienced visitations of God's power which revolutionised the scholars and students.

By the time the Convention came round again in 1906 it was apparent to those closest to Hyde that God was taking him deeper still into the mysteries of intercession. His vision was of Christ as the lamb on the throne interceding ceaselessly for us. The burden of souls weighed so heavily upon him that he frequently wept over the sins of the world—and also over the sins of believers. Others came under the spirit of intercession with him and strong men sobbed and groaned in agony over the lost; this continued all night but many of those present were never the same afterwards. They 'prayed through' until they experienced the power of God in their lives and then they broke out into joyous praise and worship. The Convention had now grown in numbers with some thirteen hundred present as well as seventy missionaries. Some had come to mock but they left humbled and divinely chastened: God was there in the midst of His people.

Not only at these special times did Hyde pray but prayer now became ever increasingly his way of life. Friends with whom he stayed thought at times that he was going to break down under the strain, but after all night sessions of prayer and praise (for Hyde had come to recognise that praise was a vital ingredient of intercession)—he would emerge in the morning fresh and smiling. He had come to understand that God was not calling him to suffer in his own strength but according to His own power. He testified that he scarcely ever felt tired even after sometimes going weeks with almost no sleep. Frequently he groaned and agonised under the burden, but he also on many occasions then experienced holy laughter as he knew that God had given him the victory in prayer.

John's Mission eventually came to recognise the very special and unique ministry of John Hyde and wisely released him for intercession. At the Sialkot Convention in 1908 he was enabled to pray and had faith that one soul would be saved every day. That was to be a definite conversion, not an inquirer, but a commitment to Christ publicly, leading to baptism.

John returned from the Convention to his district to seek for these souls and he was not disappointed. He was a great personal worker and again and again he would succeed in leading a person to Christ. Then he would get the convert on their knees confessing their sins and seeking the Saviour. He would follow it up by baptising them in the village, or by the roadside, or anywhere that would do. As the number of converts swelled so the reality of their conversion became apparent and John always made a point of lovingly embracing his new converts when next they met; this was a habit which he encouraged others to follow with fellow Christians, even with those of the lowest caste. He saw some four hundred people converted during the year, but he was still not satisfied and at the 1909 Convention after much prayer he was assured that God would give him two souls a day during the year. His ministry at these Conventions became more and more precious to those privileged to hear him. His word was with power and hundreds left the Convention renewed and empowered.

Hyde's faith was not disappointed and he saw eight hundred

precious souls gathered in during the year, but in 1910 at the Convention his heart was still not satisfied. His cry was, 'Give me souls, O God, or I die'. He took the burden not only of the lost but like Daniel and the prophets of old he identified himself with the sins of the nation and of God's people. After much prayer he finally was enabled to believe that God would give him four souls a day during the year. By now his ministry was in demand all over India and he travelled widely helping in conferences at Calcutta and Bombay—yet, side by side with this he had to endure being more misjudged and misunderstood than ever before. Some even hated him—but he accepted it all as part of the fellowship of Christ's sufferings. Throughout the 1910 Convention Hyde spent long nights in prayer, and to those nearest to him it was apparent that each year the burden grew heavier and heavier. Yet when he stood to preach he was like a prophet: his very face radiated the glory of his Lord and his hearers knew that God was speaking to them through His servant with most unusual power and authority. His themes at these Conventions were such that only someone who had suffered deeply could have ministered upon with conviction. One year it was on Paul being willing to be an anathema from Christ if only his fellow Jews could be won (Romans 9:1–3). In 1910 Hyde preached on the selfless intercession of Moses on the Mount Sinai as he sought to keep God from destroying Israel in His wrath. His hearers listened and accepted it from John because those who had been coming year after year to the Convention had witnessed the commitment of his prayer life.

If Hyde found that on any day the promised four people were not converted he could not eat or sleep. As he sought for the reason for the failure he would say that God had revealed to him that it was through want of praise in his life. He would immediately confess his failure and seek for forgiveness and the cleansing of the blood of Christ and then ask the Lord to give him the spirit of praise. As the blessing of praise was released through him so the miracle happened and the numbers of new converts would be made up. That memorable year of 1910 was his last one at Sialkot; it was his seventh year there since the inception of the Convention and every year its influence and power to spread revival far beyond the immediate area had grown. John Hyde was not the only great person of prayer involved in the Convention, but all acknowledged that he was the outstanding leader by far.

Soon after the 1910 Convention John was in Calcutta for a meeting there. During this time he began to be very unwell and the friend with whom he was staying persuaded him to see his doctor. When the doctor examined him he was staggered at what he found: John Hyde's heart was in a terrible condition and outside anything he had come across in his previous medical experience. The heart had apparently been shifted out of its natural position on the left side to a place over on the right side. He warned John that unless he changed his way of life and rested completely he would be dead in six months.

The doctor was asking the impossible of John Hyde: he had made his commitment, he had tasted of the powers of the world to come, he could no more draw back than he could deny his Saviour. Years before he had surrendered all thoughts of marriage as part of his consecration to the Christ whom he loved with all his heart, and in the same way he was quite prepared to hazard his life for Christ as he continued in intercession. In spite of physical weakness and pain he still prayed through the night on occasions.

He was due to appear at the Annual Conference of his Mission but it was clearly impossible for him to attend and he started writing out his report, but was unable even to finish that because of the pain in his head. Yet he was not sad, or downcast. The shout of victory was another essential part of John's spiritual warfare. The sword of the Spirit was seldom out of his hands and never out of his heart.

Hyde's favourite posture in the prayer room at Sialkot was lying on the carpet on his face before God. But when he was used by God to bring deliverance to believers confessing their sins, he would minister to them and pray until 'they came through' into victory and joy. Then he would be so full of joy that he would begin to clap his hands and then begin to dance with joy; soon others in the prayer room would join him until the whole place rang with the praises of God.

It transpired that one religious group was so troubled at the number of converts being made among their men by Hyde that they sent a spy to destroy Hyde. Their purpose was to expose his faults and publish them and so destroy his influence. The man posed as an inquirer and was invited by Hyde to stay in his home, but after three or four days the man fled and reported to the religious group which had sent him that he could find no fault in Hyde and that he was a truly holy person.

In March 1911, Hyde sailed from India for the last time. He was a dying man. On the way home to America he called at England and stayed for a few months with some of his missionary colleagues. He spent some precious weeks with his esteemed friend Rev J. Pengwern Jones. They planned to visit Keswick together and establish a prayer room there such as the one at Sialkot, but John was too ill to attend. But he did join with the speakers and promoters of Keswick in a two day prayer meeting at the home of Evan Hopkins. Evan Hopkins greatly appreciated Hyde's fellowship but there were some forty people present and on the second day they set aside a time to discuss the possibility of a prayer room at Keswick. Jones and Hyde were asked to share from their experience at Sialkot; Jones spoke first and was very brief, wanting to give preference to Hyde. But Hyde when he started speaking was even slower than usual. Jones was the only one who really knew Hyde. Jones knew from experience that from his manner Hyde had a special burden to share. He spoke very quietly for three or four minutes and then one of the ladies present started up a popular hymn and the message was never delivered. Hyde showed no resentment at such treatment but simply closed his eyes and prayed.

Hyde sailed for America during the summer and arrived in New York on August 11th. A medical examination revealed that he was suffering from a tumour which an operation found was malignant. He rallied after the operation and spent some time with his sister (his parents having died). He died on February 17th, 1912 and was buried in his birthplace at Carthage, Illinois on February 20th beside his parents and his brother Edmund. Before his death John Hyde had shared an experience he had some years before in India when on a day of prayer God showed him that the battle was not just in the Punjab, or in all India even, but beyond in China, Japan and Africa. He was shown how they had been thinking in narrow circles of their own countries and their own denominations, but that God was rapidly joining force to force and it was all beginning to be one great struggle, a world battle and the great triumph of Christ. It was a prophetic vision for this twentieth century.

John Hyde died with the shout of victory on his lips, 'Shout, the victory of Jesus Christ!' Holiness was the great characteristic of his life and prayer his life work. His consuming passion was his love for his Lord and Saviour Jesus Christ.

7: Rees Howells

It was a case of singing all the way as the local train to Llanelli chugged out of the station on a July morning in 1915. The crowd of well-wishers on the platform waved and sang as only Welsh people can. It seemed as though the whole town had turned out to give a great send-off to Rees and Elizabeth Howells as they left for missionary work in Africa. Nor did the singing stop when the train had left the platform far behind, because many of the locals had decided to travel with them the twenty miles to Llanelli. There the new missionary couple would have to change and catch the mainline train for London, and then the boat which would take them to darkest Africa. It was an event not to be missed, an occasion to be savoured. They sang revival hymns and choruses all the way. Rees and Elizabeth joined in but not with their usual fervour. Their hearts were still aching at having to leave their baby son, Samuel, and it would be years before they would see him again. But their minds were occupied with a more immediate problem—their fare from Llanelli to London. They had used up all their money on their missionary kit, apart from ten shillings (50p), confident that the Lord would send in the money for the journey to London before the time came for them to leave. All week they had eagerly waited for the postman to call but in vain. There was only one thing to do (for it was a principle with them never to make their needs known except to God). They would use what money they had to book them as far as Llanelli and believe God to meet the need for the remainder of the fare to London en route. But nothing had come their way except songs and good wishes.

Now here they were on the platform at Llanelli with the London train due in very shortly. Rees lifted his heart to God for guidance and help. He felt the Holy Spirit whispering into his heart to believe that God's promises are as good as cash in your pocket, and to take his place in the ticket queue at the booking office. There were about a dozen people in front of him. All too quickly they were dealt with and Rees found himself third—and still no help. The devil was very busy telling him that he was going to make a fool of himself and that when his turn came he would have to walk by. Suddenly a man stepped out of the crowd on the platform and said that he could not wait any longer, he had to leave and go and open his shop, but he wanted to shake Rees by the hand. On doing so, he gave Rees thirty shillings (£1.50) which was sufficient for their fare! Rees and Elizabeth sang all the way to London— they had proved God once again in the most practical way. It had taken years before Rees had come to such a place of faith and God had trained him in a very tough school—but neither he nor Elizabeth had any regrets.

Rees Howells was Welsh from head to toe and that represented quite a lot of Welshman for he was almost six feet tall, broad-shouldered, lean and tough from his years as a coalminer. Underneath his broad square-cut forehead was set a pair of clear, penetrating eyes which sparkled with life, frequently twinkled with fun (he loved a joke), but often burned with the far-away look of Welsh mysticism. His father, Thomas Howells, was both an iron-worker and a coal-miner, and lived in a little white-washed cottage on the Llandilo Road in the mining village of Brynamman, South Wales. His wife, Margaret bore him a marvellous family of three girls and eight boys, and Rees was born the middle and sixth child on 10th October 1879. Life was hard but happy for the Howells. Thomas moved from the iron works to the coal mine to earn more money for his ever growing family. Things finally became easier for them all when he managed to open a shoe shop in the village for the sale and repair of footwear. Education at the village school was then compulsory to the age of thirteen, but Rees left at twelve with the contrivance of the manager of the iron works who offered him a job. He worked there for ten years along with his brothers.

Rees loved to visit his grandparents up on the Black Mountain at Pentwyn. They had both been converted in the famous 1859 revival which had swept Wales and the rest of the United Kingdom. Rees loved the atmosphere in their home; he sensed the presence of God there, but though he was 'religious' and attended chapel regularly with the rest of the family, maintained upright morals and even went to the prayer meetings, he had never been truly converted.

Rees' cousin, Evan Lewis, along with several others from the area, had emigrated to America and was earning more money than had ever been possible in Wales. At twenty-two years of age, Rees left Wales to join his cousin in America and make his fortune in that land of opportunity—then retire early! He got a job in a tin mill in Pittsburgh and joined a church, never missing a prayer meeting. Rees was pleased with life in general as he succeeded in making very good money in America, and pleased with himself in particular as he was making a favourable impression on the minister and the congregation. However, one day cousin Evan Lewis spoiled it all by daring to ask him if he was 'born again'! Rees was nonplussed: he had no idea what his cousin was talking about. All he knew was that somehow the question deeply disturbed him. He defended himself by saying that his life was as good as Evan's and that he was a Christian and that was all there was to it. But Evan was not deterred so easily and over the next few weeks he persisted with his probing questions and Rees began to argue with him. In the end Rees decided that rather than quarrel with Evan it would be best to move elsewhere. He moved to a place called Martin's Ferry about a hundred miles away, but he was not allowed to leave without a parting shot from Evan, who said he would not mind Rees leaving if only he were born again . . . Rees could not get the words out of his mind.

Over the next weeks, however, Rees read a book which helped him to realise that although he was religious he did not have a real relationship with God.

Then suddenly Rees went down with the dreaded typhoid fever. At twenty-three years of age he found himself facing death for the first time and he was desperately afraid. For five months he lived in the fear of death. He was no longer concerned about making money, only about making his peace with God, if only he knew how. When Rees was sufficiently recovered he travelled back to Pittsburgh to see if his cousin could help him, but unfortunately Evan was not skilled enough in Christian counselling to lead him to Christ. Rees decided to move again and he settled at Connellsville, Pennsylvania. Shortly afterwards a converted Jew, Maurice Reuben, came there to conduct an evangelistic crusade in a Methodist church and Rees went along to hear him. Listening to the evangelist's amazing testimony Rees saw the cross of Christ in a new way. The evangelist belonged to a wealthy Jewish family who owned a very large department store. Through the witness of one of the buyers Reuben had accepted Christ, even though he realised that it would probably cost him his wife, his family fortune, and everything else. In an attempt to silence Reuben his family had him arrested and declared insane. In the mental asylum he had a vision of the crucifixion which strengthened his resolve to serve Christ no matter what the cost. Through the intervention of Christian friends he was ultimately released and became a very effective evangelist.

Until he heard Reuben's testimony Rees had kept one last line of defence. He always stumbled over the fact that the lives of many so-called born-again Christians were no better, or even as good, as his own. He said in his heart that if ever he could see a person living the Sermon on the Mount he would yield and be 'born again'. However, as he listened to the evangelist's story he knew that God was confronting him with such a life. When the evangelist went on to describe the crucifixion in graphic detail, Rees also saw it in a deeper way than ever before. He broke down completely and wept. Without reserve he yielded his whole life to Christ and at that moment he knew what it was to be born again. He later testified that up to that moment he had only experienced a historical Christ: now he had a personal Saviour. Within a very short time he was planning to return home to Wales; he now had a new ambition in life and not even the tempting offer of a large pay rise by his works manager could entice him to stay in America.

God had clearly intended Rees to arrive home at that time, in the significant year of the great Welsh revival, 1904. This was an event which left an indelible impression upon the newly converted Rees Howells. Here he saw the power of God in action. Whatever he had heard from his grandparents about the famous 1859 revival was now being re-enacted before his very eyes. The chapels were filled to overflowing day after day with singing, praying, praising people. Multitudes of nominal Christians, religious church-goers as he himself had been, were transformed into born again believers. Crowds of hardened sinners were gloriously converted. The atmosphere in the coal mines was changed. The miners sang as the descended the deep shafts. At work they showed such gentleness that many of the pit ponies, unused to kind treatment, refused to work!

The police cells were empty; crime was reduced to a minimum; pubs were closing down; but prayer meetings proliferated. There was great conviction of sin: the Holy Spirit was at work. Young Evan Roberts, one of God's great instruments in the revival, urged people to forgive everyone from their hearts and to obey the promptings of God's Spirit.

Rees discerned that obedience to the Spirit and open confession of Christ brought the blessing of God down upon the people. He revelled in those days of heaven upon earth.

Although but a young convert himself, he quickly matured as he experienced the visitation from God in those days. As the revival subsided he was greatly concerned over the need to establish and strengthen the new converts.

On his return Rees had settled in again with his parents in the family home and taken up a job as a miner at the coal-face, but all his spare time was given to furthering the revival. Caring for the converts drove him and his friends to the realisation of their own need for spiritual power. Consequently a large party of them decided to attend the famous Llandrindod Wells Convention in the summer of 1906. The first speaker was the outstanding exponent of Keswick 'deeper life' teaching, Rev Evan Hopkins; his text was Ephesians 2:1–6, and his theme was on the believer being raised and seated with Christ in the heavenly realms. On the train going to the Convention, a voice within Rees whispered: 'When you return you will be a new man', which puzzled him tremendously. What could it mean? He was about to find out.

On the second day of the Convention, Evan Hopkins preached about the Holy Spirit being a Person, the Third Person of the Godhead. All this was new to Rees and he drank it in eagerly. But as the truth and its full implications dawned upon him a battle began in his heart. The Holy Spirit was demanding his unconditional surrender, and he went out into a field to be alone with God. It took five days for him to make the irrevocable decision to take the step to go forward with God, for the Holy Spirit had made it very clear to him that there could be no going back afterwards. Things which were permissible to others would not be so for him; he was to be different. The Spirit of God convicted Rees about his love of money his ambition and his reputation. The fifth day of this searching was Friday and the Holy Spirit emphasised that his surrender would mean the end of living for self in any form; he would have to live for others and follow Christ completely. Furthermore the Spirit impressed upon him that his decision must be made by six o'clock that evening! Rees pleaded for more time but the Holy Spirit made it absolutely clear that six was the deadline. At ten minutes to six, Rees found himself wanting to do it but unable to do so. At five to six the Holy Spirit whispered into his heart, offering to help him to be made willing. At one minute to six Rees looked up at the clock and realised that time was running out. He bowed his head and said, 'Lord, I am willing'.

What followed was too sacred for words. Rees experienced such a filling of the Spirit as he never dreamed possible. When he returned from Llandrindod Wells he was indeed changed into another man. Rees very quickly realised that although the crisis was past, the process of the Spirit sanctifying his life and teaching him the secrets of spiritual power had only just begun. During those five days he had lost seven pounds in weight, so fierce and real was the conflict.

The first lesson he had to learn was the secret of prevailing prayer. Until then Rees' praying had been as general and as haphazard as that of many Christians; now the Spirit began to teach him that it was to be specific and definite, and only as He Himself indicated.

An early lesson the Holy Spirit taught him was that he must never ask God to answer a prayer through others, if the means to answer it lay within his own power—especially in the realm of finance.

The Holy Spirit's training ground for Rees was his own village and his tough, unsparing apprenticeship was to last for six long years. As Rees gave himself to prayer on his return from that memorable Llandrindod Wells Convention he found to his astonishment that God was placing on his conscience a dirty, down-and-out, alcoholic tramp, called Will Battery, who had been living rough for two years. The challenge was to pray for this man to receive salvation and return to sound sense. It was a sad case—Will's troubles had begun with meningitis which had left him physically weakened and badly affected. He had come to the village to live with his uncle but had started drinking to alleviate his misery and had become an alcoholic. Will's nights were spent on the warm boilers of the local tin mill. Rees took Will on his heart and found the Holy Spirit filling it with God's love for this poor, depraved creature. He made Will his friend; he spent all his Sundays with him and walked around the village with him—to the stares and strange looks of many. Rees even spent Christmas Day with Will in the boiler house of the tin mill! His mother packed a basket of Christmas goodies which Will scoffed eagerly.

Rees' efforts were rewarded when Will asked if he could accompany Rees to the little house group in the evening. It took three years of patience and prayer before Will was fully rehabilitated with a job, lodgings, and clothes. However, the day finally came when to the astonishment of the chapel-goers, Will came and took his place among them, 'clothed and in his right mind'. God put the seal on this conversion when Rees was able to persuade Will to return home to his mother who had prayed for him for years.

A second lesson God had in store for Rees was on what he came to term 'princely giving'. As he was praying one morning the Lord brought before him a notorious character who had been recently converted in the revival. His name was Jim Stakes; he had a terrible reputation for wickedness of all kinds, and drink had dragged him and his family down to the depths of poverty. His conversion had created a sensation in the village. Rees found himself interceding in the power of the Spirit for this man; and he realised that he was in a battle for the soul of this new convert, whom he had met but once. If the devil could reclaim him it would be a terrible setback for the revival. Rees promised God he would do anything to help. The same evening Jim knocked on his door and told Rees that at ten in the morning while he was working down the mine, Rees had been brought before him in a very real way. Rees was impressed because that was the very time he had been praying for Jim. As he listened to Jim's tale of woe it transpired that through his drinking he was two years behind with the rent and the bailiffs were coming to take possession of his furniture. Rees promised to give him a year's rent and said he would see if a friend would give the rest. As he went upstairs to fetch the money the Holy Spirit whispered into his heart, 'Why are you only giving half?' In a moment Rees obeyed and came downstairs with the full amount needed. As he pressed it into Jim's hands a great joy flooded his soul. This 'princely giving' softened the heart of Jim's wife who was still unconverted and she surrendered her life to Christ when Rees visited their home the following Sunday. It marked a new breakthrough in the district. They started a house meeting in their home every Saturday and Sunday evening, led by Rees and his friends, and some of the worst characters in the area were converted.

Spiritually, Rees was especially close to his Uncle Dick, who had been an invalid for twenty-six years. He was an exceptional Christian with a meek, submissive spirit. He was unable to walk more than a few yards, nor was he able to concentrate on reading except for very short spells, but he spent hours daily in prayer, and was one of many such intercessors who had prayed for years for the revival. When it came he rejoiced and he was especially thrilled that his nephew Rees had returned from America a born again believer. They were kindred spirits and became very close to each other. Despite the fact that not all Rees' friends were sympathetic to his Llandrindod experience Rees knew he had to tell his uncle about his experience of the Holy Spirit. But how would he receive it? To his joy he found his uncle's heart and mind open to the truth and after some three weeks of earnest seeking he also entered into a deeper life in the Spirit and became Rees's chief prayer partner.

The next challenge the Holy Spirit brought before Rees was a neighbouring village called Tairgwaith which had been by-passed completely in the revival and could not boast a single Christian or a place of worship. The Holy Spirit impressed upon Rees that these people had not even been moved by

great preaching in the revival and He was calling Rees to so identify himself with them that he must be willing to suffer many
things in order to win them to Christ. When Rees and a handful
of his close friends visited the village one Sunday morning they
were appalled to find the people drinking, gambling, and
indulging in all kinds of games and activities, outside in the
open. They felt it justified its nickname of Hell-Fire Row.

In the first house they visited, the woman burned her bread
baking in the oven through talking to them. Rees was unaware
of this at the time but when he heard what had happened he
returned to apologise and gave the woman a sovereign (a
pound gold coin). The news quickly spread that this crowd of
young people, all workers like themselves and not
'professional preachers', backed up their words with practical
deeds of kindness. The woman and her husband opened up
their home for meetings and these two former drunkards
became the first converts. A bridgehead was now established
but the Holy Spirit whispered into Rees' heart that he was to
become responsible for the needs of everyone in the village. It
was a tall order; no longer could he call anything his own.

A breakthrough came when the ringleader of the drinkers
was converted. Rees had prayed much for an opportunity to
touch this ringleader and it came when the man got involved
in a court case. Rees felt the Lord wanted him to offer to settle
the case out of court for the man. The man was only too
willing and the other party were also ready to accept the
compensation which Rees paid on the man's behalf. Such a
demonstration of practical Christianity broke this hardened
sinner and he started attending the meetings. Within a very
short time more than twelve followed their ringleader and
surrendered to Christ. Rees held meetings five nights every
week and the other two nights they spent visiting the converts
and other homes. The work spread rapidly, and Rees had to
pay out an increasing percentage of his savings and earnings as
he faithfully played out the role of local 'philanthropist
extraordinaire'. In record time he was down to his last pound.

Strangely enough, that was when Rees found himself fighting his biggest battle. It was easier to give a hundred pounds out of his plenty than to give away his last pound and for the first time in fifteen years find himself penniless.

At last Rees gained victory over his reluctance to give his all, and with the surrender of his last pound came the revelation from God that he could now claim the 'hundredfold' as promised by the Lord Jesus to His disciples: '. . . Everyone that has forsaken houses . . . or lands . . . for my name's sake shall receive an hundredfold' (Matthew 19:29). God was teaching His servant the secrets of the life of faith and in Rees He found a ready pupil. Rees realised that God Himself was now his resource and the Bank of Heaven was open worldwide, twenty-four hours every day! Nevertheless it was not very long before his new position of faith was tested to the hilt. A strike was threatened and as the previous stoppage of work had lasted eight months Rees was under no delusions about the demands God was asking of him. In prayer the Holy Spirit impressed upon him that he was to be responsible for feeding the village throughout the threatened strike, which could last months. It could mean Rees having to obtain credit for up to a hundred pounds from the local grocers, on behalf of the villagers, who were denied it themselves due to past untrustworthiness. Rees prayed earnestly about this challenge the Sunday night before the strike was due to begin. In the meeting that night he boldly announced that even if the strike lasted nine months not one of them would go hungry, and he would be responsible for supplying their needs. Not surprisingly the meeting erupted in a great burst of praise and thanksgiving which could not be contained.

Next morning Rees met a local agnostic who was always criticising the church, calling it useless and also accusing the mining authorities of being responsible for the strike. Rees asked him what he was doing to help the people who would suffer in the strike, and went on to tell him what God had told him to promise. The man was dumbstruck for once. Just then the newsboy came along with the newspaper carrying the welcome news that the strike had been settled, but the testimony had been made to the glory of God and Rees's faith continued to grow. Every night, for two years, rain or shine, he walked the two miles each way to that village after a hard day's work as a miner cutting coal deep in the bowels of the earth.

In common with other mining families, the Howells boys were fed four meals a day by their mother, 'to keep their strength up'. It came as a real shock to Rees' system when God brought to his attention for the first time the need to pray and fast. That lunchtime he went upstairs to his bedroom and got down on his knees, but found prayer impossible. Gradually the aroma of his mother's cooking wafted upstairs. She called him but he told her he was not having any lunch. Like the good mother she was she was soon back, calling and telling him it would only take a little while to have it and it was ready. It was all too much for him and down he came to tuck in to the meal. But how he suffered afterwards! Rees knew he had failed. Full of remorse he went up the small mountain behind the village and walked for miles, weeping and confessing his weakness. Next day he won the battle of the midday meal and did not take lunch for many more days. The victory was his; he was learning the power of adding fasting to prayer when prompted to do so by the Holy Spirit.

Out of that period of fasting from his lunch, God gave him a burden for the tramps who wandered around the area in droves, because of the unemployment situation. He was to put Isaiah 58 into action: 'to feed the hungry . . . care for the poor, and clothe the naked'; that was God's chosen fast. The same day a tramp came into their meeting. They welcomed him with open arms; they fed him, clothed him, provided him with lodgings and got a job for him. The news of this Welsh Utopia spread like wildfire and they found themselves having to cope with a steady stream of down-and-outs. Not one was turned away. They found themselves loving these people and Rees felt the Holy Spirit challenging him to identify more closely with them. As the government hostels only provided tramps with two meals a day of bread, cheese, and soup, God challenged Rees to eat similarly. The fasting from his mid-day meals had prepared the way for him to cut down further but the real problem was persuading his mother to feed him less. She eventually agreed but Rees found his soup the thickest and most nourishing in the whole of Wales! Her worries proved groundless: Rees flourished on his two meals a day taken at 6.30 am and 5.30 pm; his health actually improved and he kept to this diet for two-and-a-half years.

Caring for an endless stream of tramps soon exhausted the funds of the little mission, and they were thrown on God to see what He would do. They soon proved the Lord's faithfulness as they discovered that it did not matter how many came, His provision never failed. They paid the grocery bill every two weeks and all the workers emptied their pockets; again and again they found they had exactly the right amount. It happened too frequently for it to be mere coincidence—they knew it had to be God's doing and their faith grew by leaps and bounds. At one time they had as many as sixteen tramps in the meeting, all cleaned up, newly clothed, and fed; but most important of all many of them came to a real experience of Christ's saving power. Not that they were without their disappointments. It was not unknown for a tramp to go off and pawn or sell the new suit they had just given him and return for another. Even harder to bear was when the conversion of some proved to be spurious. It nearly broke their hearts but they were learning all the time.

Rees was now ready for the next grade in God's school for intercessors. As Rees and his friends were passing a group of intoxicated women one day, he wondered how they could find the power to change such people. Rees felt an immediate stirring in his heart and as he prayed he felt that the Holy Spirit was guiding him to pick out the ringleader of the women, (who had a terrible reputation in addition to being a

confirmed drunkard) and pray for her to be saved by
Christmas Day. During this time he had no contact with the
woman as the Spirit of God made it clear that his only means
of reaching out to her was to be through prayer. He was
learning the secret of 'binding the strong man' as Jesus
described Satan in Matthew 12:29. As he waited on God and
searched His Word on his knees, the Holy Spirit quickened
the promise of Jesus: 'If you abide in Me and My words abide
in you, you shall ask what you will and it shall be done unto
you' (John 15:7).

In the weeks that followed Rees interceded for this woman
and as he did so was taken to a deeper level of prayer, which
involved a great searching of his own heart. He learned to
'abide' by spending a set time every day waiting upon God,
and obeying every prompting and command of the Spirit. All
the time he became more and more aware that he was engaged
in a battle with the enemy of souls and the powers of darkness.
It was real spiritual warfare. After six weeks the Holy Spirit
revealed to him that he could expect to see some indication of
a move in this woman's life. The same night she arrived at an
open air meeting. Rees rejoiced but still made no attempt to
contact her. As he continued with his intercession he was
thrilled when she started to attend the house meeting. The
Holy Spirit made it clear to him that now it was a matter for
praising rather than praying, although the woman had made
no outward move of actually coming to Christ. There were
still six weeks to Christmas Day and Rees spent those weeks
praising in faith. He could hardly wait for Christmas Day—
her salvation was to be his Christmas present! The woman
came to the meeting but it was unusually noisy and constantly
disrupted because of a high number of excited children there.
Nevertheless in the middle of the meeting this notorious
woman went down on her knees and cried to God for mercy.
Her conversion proved to be lasting and Rees knew that he
had graduated still further in the secrets of prayer.

The manager of one of the local works had co-operated with

Rees' group in their work among the tramps by providing jobs. His wife had been converted but he himself was quite godless and proud of it. They began to pray for him and soon he invited Rees and his friends to his house for a meeting. They kept it very low-key and just sang a few hymns and had a happy time together. He invited them back the following week and they were more open but still careful not to press too hard. Rees eventually felt that the time had come for them all to claim the victory for this man's salvation, sure that they had already gained the place of power by their intercession for him. The phrase which became part of his prayer vocabulary was 'the gained position of intercession'; very much as soldiers would describe their taking a key position in a battle. The manager invited them back a third time. That week they all tried to ensure that they kept in the place of 'abiding', allowing no unbelief to enter their hearts or any hindrance to arise in their spirits.

On their way to the manager's house next week they walked past a number of houses. Suddenly, Rees heard the Holy Spirit speaking in his heart and directing him to go and knock on one of the doors! He dismissed the thought and walked on but stopped after a few hundred yards. He now knew enough of the Lord's dealings with him to recognise that this was not anything of his own fancy but a definite leading of God's Spirit. He duly returned taking one of his friends with him. Rees' knock on the door produced a little girl who, without any questions invited them in. There they found a very sick woman dying with tuberculosis. As soon as she saw Rees she lifted her thin arms and told them that they had come in answer to her prayers—she had been praying all day that God would bring Rees to the house. Facing death she knew that although she had been a church member for years she was not sure of her salvation. It was beautifully easy for Rees to point her to the Saviour and immediately she received an assurance that her sins were forgiven and she was filled with joy. When they eventually arrived at the manager's home they apologised and explained what had happened. As they told the story the manager fell on his knees so suddenly that he pulled his chair over on top of him, but disregarding this and everything else he cried out to God to save him. The incident of the woman with T.B. had touched his heart in a way nothing else could have done.

Over the years in the village the Holy Spirit continued to shape and refine this chosen vessel. Rees found that things did not get any easier; the testings got hotter, the trials much fiercer. He discovered somewhat to his surprise that there was more to learn about giving. God taught him that he was to regard himself as a steward: in future he was not to spend even the smallest amount without permission. For the next eighteen months he spent nothing except on absolute bare necessities. The principle was that while there were people in God's world without the necessities of life he was to live as simply as possible and give all he could as God directed. The devil really tempted him over this further surrender of his fiscal rights, but Rees knew a transaction had been made with God. The Holy Spirit revealed that far from being restricted he was now in a position where God could pour His provision through him to those in need. He became utterly dead to money; its hold was broken completely. He began to understand what living by faith meant.

Learning about healing proved costly indeed. One day, the woman who had burned her bread on the day Rees and his friends first entered the village fell ill with T.B. In her dying condition she asked Rees about divine healing, and he promised he would pray about it but confessed to a certain amount of fear as he did so. For six months Rees sought God and searched the Scriptures until he came to believe that physical healing as well as forgiveness of sins was in the atonement of Christ. Intercession for him had come to mean identification with the sufferer and he wondered what it would entail to intercede for this victim of tuberculosis. He came to the place in his intercession where he felt that he had to be willing to take this woman's disease in his own body. The woman herself believed she would be healed and said so. It was already something of a miracle that she was still alive and she did seem to be making some progress. As she had several children dependent on her it seemed right to ask God for a miracle, and Rees had faith that it would happen. However, on the evening before Good Friday the woman shattered him by saying that she now believed that she was going to die. Rees tried to encourage her to hold on in faith: as everyone was expecting God to raise her up her death would be a terrible blow. As he prayed that night he felt that God was actually asking him to so identify with the woman that he must be willing not only to take her T.B. but to die in her place if need be. He went to bed without praying and rose determined not to go any further with this costly business of intercession. It was a dark night for him but eventually he came to the point where he was willing to die if only this woman might live. Rees then ran the two miles to the woman's house, full of joy, certain that God was going to heal the woman and take him home to heaven that very night in her place. Needless to say the sick woman refused to pray for this—she felt that Rees' life was much more important than hers.

Over the next few months both Rees and the sick woman entered into a glorious new experience of God as God's glory filled the sickroom, although every day Rees sincerely thought he may die. When the woman did eventually die it was a real shock to him but the Spirit of God assured him that his intercession had been accepted: God was calling him to be a living martyr instead of a dying one. He knew that everyone in the district would regard this death as a failure, but in his heart he believed that God had shown him not to defend himself in any way. The funeral instead of being a depressing affair of defeat turned out to be a victory and finished like a revival meeting. The woman's dying words had been ones of assurance: she told her friends to tell Rees that she could not wait for him as the Saviour had come for her and she wanted to go. She then shook hands with all her friends around the bedside and departed this life.

Sadly, however, the minister conducting the funeral tried to use the occasion to criticise Rees and his friends, quoting from Job 13:1–5 to the effect that 'they were all forgers of lies . . . .' Hundreds had gathered round the graveside but when Rees followed with a few words of testimony about the way this woman's life had changed since becoming a Christian, and told them of her trimphant death-bed scene, the atmosphere was lifted. People started to sing as in the revival; soon they were waving their handkerchiefs and giving glory to God.

Rees Howell's life work was to be mainly that of intercession; he was now at the 'postgraduate' stage yet still finding himself being stretched to new limits. At this period the only inspiration he found apart from the Bible was in the life of George Müller and the life of Madame Guyon and her writings. He came to see that a true intercessor is committed to gaining his objective even though it cost him everything, including his life.

Although the woman with T.B. had eventually died Rees soon realised that through this experience he had reached a deeper understanding of divine healing, which was soon put to the test. One day he heard that a man in the village, the father of ten children and their only breadwinner was desperately ill and dying. When Rees called at the house he found the man's wife in tears and her husband unconscious. He went out into the fields and prayed and wept, but when he returned to the house he heard God's voice telling him that the man was not to die but live! He told the man's wife but she did not believe him. It was a testing experience for Rees but the promised deliverance came and the man was healed to the amazement of many.

This incident was quickly followed by another case of a woman dying after childbirth and given up by the doctor. She had a large family and had been one of their finest converts.

Rees sought God over this, and again the voice of God came into his heart assuring him she would be healed. He returned to the house to tell the woman's husband, and together with half-a-dozen of the children they gathered round her bed praying and praising God. Within a short time the woman took a turn for the better and was soon completely healed! Many healings followed, and Rees found himself with a new sensitivity to the voice of God in the realm of divine healing.

Their little mission was now prospering and growing with Rees as the leader along with a close friend called Johnny Lewis. One day as Johnny was preaching in the open air Rees discovered that there was jealousy in his heart because of his friend's exceptional preaching ability. He had to do some deep repenting over this jealousy before he found release.

Through his visits to the Llandrindod Wells conventions every year, Rees had become friendly with some notable people, one of whom was Mr John Gosset of London. Gosset was very impressed with Rees, having heard him preach with unusual power, and wanted him to meet Lord Radstock and Sir Robert Anderson in London. A message Rees gave on one occasion was a special help and blessing to Lord Radstock who had come into quite a healing ministry but had experienced an apparent 'failure' in the same way as Rees, when his daughter died.

Gosset's invitation for Rees to come to London was received by Rees with some pride. It was really something special for a miner like himself to be invited to meet some of society's élite. During the following weeks, Rees found himself with a new prayer battle on his hands. Some of the converted drunkards were still having a problem with alcohol. They set themselves to bind the strong man in order to set these victims free. Rees found himself so busy, working full time as a miner, then involved with the mission every evening, that it was a problem to find time to pray. He loved to spend his time walking the two miles to the mission in prayer. God's presence was so real to him as he walked in the open air that he felt he had to uncover his head just as he would in church. He carried his cap as he prayed, but when he came to the village street among people he would quickly don his cap again in keeping with the social convention of his day. It was unknown for any respectable man to walk out in public without a hat. Rees resolved that he must keep in a spirit of prayer all day but the crunch came when he felt that the Holy Spirit was telling him that he must be *hatless* all day too! So strong was the social convention about wearing hats that no self-respecting male would ever walk down the street without one. When Sunday came Rees hoped that all the family would have left the house before him, but sure enough there was his mother at the foot of the stairs brushing his Sunday hat in readiness for him. He had to pass by and go out without it.

Rees died inwardly over this issue. He found it a bigger battle than fasting. The whole village stared at this hatless figure walking down the village street on Sunday morning. It was a reproach to the whole Howells family too and that Rees found hard to bear. However, he found that the worst was yet to come, for as he departed for London he knew that God was calling him to go hatless to the capital! Rees felt bitter shame, knowing full well what Mr Gosset's reaction would be, moving in his social circle—it would be counted an insult. Mr Gosset was a proud man and he blushed with embarrassment as he rode with the hatless Rees in an open carriage through the great streets of London. He made Rees walk a few yards behind him on the street—he just could not bear to be seen with a hatless companion. Afterwards, however, he confessed that God used it to break his pride which he knew was a stumbling block in his life. Eventually God vindicated Rees and owned his ministry in such a way that Gosset became his life-long friend, and together they entered into a prayer-pact for Gosset's backslidden son and prayed for years until he was finally restored. Before he left London, Rees and Gosset were both able to have a good laugh about hats—indeed they laughed for hours over that and other things—for Rees loved a good joke and had a wonderful sense of humour.

Back home at the village Rees discovered that God was calling him to withdraw completely from active participation in the mission and give himself to intercession. He was to resign from the mission and hand it over to Lewis. The mission had been very dear to him and it was a costly sacrifice. He was not even to attend the meetings but every night when he came home from work he was to pray from 6 pm to 9 pm. He read the Bible through on his knees and the Holy Spirit opened the Scriptures to him as never before. Rees' behaviour sent many rumours round the village but he was to remain silent. God knew and that was all that mattered. Every night as soon as he entered his room Rees knew that he was in the presence of God. Prayer became a heavenly experience.

Then came the last test: God called Rees to take the vow of a Nazarite as set out in Numbers 6:2–6. It would mean the end of haircutting and shaving until God released him. Rees was now just thirty years of age. What would his five brothers think of this long-haired monster? Even more to the point what about his mother and father?—it would be enough to kill them with shame. It would be easier if he could leave home while under this vow but as he prayed he knew that God would not allow that. If only he could be allowed to explain his actions to them, but the Holy Spirit had laid a vow of silence upon him in this respect. The longer his hair and beard grew, the more the stories about crazy Rees flew round the village. Even some of his dearest friends thought he really had gone too far this time. One who stood by him was his dear friend Elizabeth Jones, even though it seemed to both of them that any hopes of marraige had gone because of God's leading in their lives.

Rees stuck to his vow for six months and before the end God had vindicated him and even in the streets many of the men touched their hat to him as he passed; they sensed the presence of God in him like an ancient prophet come to life.

After six months God released Rees and his mother was overjoyed to hear that he was going to the barber's! He felt, however, that God was giving him the choice to continue with his intercession for another four months during which among other things he was to intercede for the child widows of India. The pathetic state of these unwanted girls who were bought or stolen by Temple women to be 'married' to the Temple god, touched his heart. He began to pray for them but soon found that God wanted him to identify with these poor widows by living as they did on the most frugal diet: he was to eat one meal of oats every two days, with a little milk. Needless to say, Rees was relieved that the Lord had indicated that he was free to leave home for this, knowing that his mother would never have allowed it!

This intercession lasted several months and finished with a period when Rees took only one meal every three days and was rounded off with a fast for fifteen days. God gave him the assurance that his intercession had been answered and also a word that He was going to heal Rees' invalid Uncle Dick, who was still living on the Black Mountain! At the first opportunity Rees went to share this great news with his uncle, who in turn sought God about the matter and received the further revelation that his healing would take place in four-and-a-half months' time on May 15th. They knew that they had to declare this openly in faith, though many shook their heads in disbelief and pitied the poor invalid who was allowing himself to be led astray by his nephew. Two weeks later it seemed that the critics were right as Uncle Dick took a grave turn for the worse and was in bed for a month. Neither Rees nor his uncle prayed, as they felt this would indicate unbelief; instead they praised God and Uncle Dick started preparing himself for the public service God was going to give him after he was healed. What a test of faith and trust! After all, Dick had now been an invalid for thirty years.

Uncle Dick informed Rees that God had told him the significance of May 15th was that it was Pentecost Sunday.

He was to be healed at 5.00 am and was to walk the three miles to and from the chapel. Rees was to leave the district and not visit his uncle again until after the healing in case anyone should give the glory to man and not to God alone. They chuckled together at the wisdom of this little bit of heavenly plotting. The departure of Rees was a signal for many to gossip that he had gone only to avoid being around when his uncle's healing did not transpire on the named day.

On Saturday, May 14th, Uncle Dick was as ill as ever. Every night he had to get up in the early hours to relieve the pain of lying too long. At 2.00 am on Sunday morning he got back in bed to be taunted by insidious whispers of the enemy telling him that nothing was going to happen. He fell into a deep sleep. When he awoke as the clock was chiming five he found himself perfectly healed! Uncle Dick shouted for the family to join him. The miracle filled them with awe. Setting off a little later in the morning to walk to church the devil could not resist a last whispered suggestion that he should take a walking stick just in case. Uncle Dick dimissed it immediately and strode off to church where his presence created great wonderment and joyous thanksgiving. Rees was only ten miles away so his uncle sent a message to him about his healing but the messenger failed to deliver it and Rees did not hear of the miracle until late on Monday night. But Rees believed without seeing or hearing and his faith and patience were rewarded. Uncle Dick became an honorary home-mission worker and in the next five years visited every home in the area. He never had another day's illness until he died.

Throughout this whole period Rees was still working fulltime as a coal-miner. Then one day when he was out meditating in the solitude of his beloved Black Mountain, the Lord called him to give up his work and devote himself entirely to prayer and intercession, trusting God to supply his every need. Before this period began the Lord permitted him a month's holiday which he was to spend in pure worship. Rees spent that precious month on the lonely mountain revelling in the presence of his Lord; worshipping him in spirit and truth. He made no intercession: it was all praise and worship. During the ensuing months he proved God's faithfulness in providing his 'wages' as surely as the mine had done, and insisted on paying his mother for his keep as usual.

One day, Joe Evans, one of the young converts who had been involved with Rees from the beginning, suffered a lung haemorrhage and was ordered into a sanatorium. After five months he was no better and his doctor advised him to live in a tent on the Black Mountain for a couple of months, and this he did, but he did not improve. The doctor said his only hope of surviving the Welsh winter was to go to the tropics, but Joe's father was poor and upset at the doctor prescribing a cure which was beyond their means. The same day, Rees received a cheque for £320! Joe's father, who was not a Christian, broke down when Rees offered to pay for Joe to go to Madeira. In the event someone had to accompany Joe as he was not fit to travel alone and Rees knew that God was directing him to go along to nurse and care for Joe. Typically Rees had Joe put up in the best hotel while he stayed in the basement of a missionary's house—which was riddled with insects. Rees had to battle to love this most unloveable missionary character who treated him so shabbily, but alone on the hills of Madeira he prayed and the Lord reminded him that the sermon on the mount teaches us to pray for those that use us wrongly. He prayed until God filled his heart with a real, deep, genuine love for the man. It was another victory.

After two months, however, Joe was still showing no improvement—in fact he was in a state of collapse and seemed to be dying. Rees earnestly sought God in prayer and the now familiar inner voice assured him that within a month Joe would be healed. He immediately wrote three letters home declaring this to his family, Joe's father, and his special friend, Elizabeth Jones. The missionary with whom Rees was staying suggested that Joe should see a specialist and Rees, who believed God used natural means as well as miracles to bring about healing readily agreed. Rees footed the bill of the specialist who confirmed the hopelessness of Joe's case. When Joe's mother received Rees's letter declaring that God was going to heal her son, she showed it to the doctor at the sanatorium who had dealt with Joe's case. He laughed in unbelief when he read it and said the day it ever happened he would become a Christian.

Rees urged Joe to pray himself for the Lord to reveal to him the exact time of his healing, as had happened with Uncle Dick. Joe did so and shared with Rees that the time given him was 6.00 am on a Saturday exactly a month from the day the promise was given. They both agreed to send a cable to Joe's father on that day. The day came, and Rees could hardly sleep that night with excitement. At 6.00 am Joe came into his bedroom looking very miserable: there was no change in his condition. Immediately Rees heard that inner voice of the Holy Spirit asking whether he was still going to send the cable? It was Rees's turn to ask Joe to pray for him—which really perplexed the invalid but he dutifully obeyed. For an hour Rees wrestled with the problem. Would he send the cable without any outward evidence of Joe's healing, depending solely by faith upon God's word? After praying he went down to the telegraph office and despatched the cable bearing the one word message: 'Victory'. As he left the office he found his hands were perspiring with the tension.

A full day passed before God showed His hand: as Rees and Joe were sitting in front of the hotel waiting for their lunch, without any warning the power of God came down upon Joe and he was healed on the spot. Joe danced for joy! Suddenly he was transformed in a moment from a dying man to a man full of life and energy. Joe then challenged Rees to a race and beat him! In fact they spent the afternoon running races. The missionary Rees lived with was deeply moved when Joe came to the service later in the afternoon and described the marvellous miracle. What a send off they received when two days later they sailed for home. On returning Joe's doctor from the sanatorium examined him and pronounced him cured with not a trace of the disease to be found. True to his word Joe's doctor who had earlier laughed in unbelief was in chapel on Sunday for the first time.

Needless to say, there was a final test for Rees when he suddenly found himself coughing blood. Had *he* contracted T.B.? Was this the price for the miracle and was this what identification with the sufferer meant? He submitted himself entirely to God's hands and found himself at peace. After a few days it transpired that the trouble was very minor but Rees had 'passed his finals' in the school of faith.

Soon after his return from Madeira, Rees sensed that God was now leading him in more normal paths. On December 21st, 1910 he married the faithful Elizabeth Hannah Jones who had stuck by him through thick and thin. It was a perfect union of two very special people whose love for each other and for the Lord had been more than proved. Both of them were agreed upon 'the life of faith', trusting God to meet their every need as they remained in His will.

Rees spent three months preaching in America in 1911. On his return to Wales, he felt a definite leading to return to attending meetings again, but where? As he prayed he was certain that they should not go back to the mission but to the Congregational Chapel. After the Revival something of a gulf had come between the many new missions and the established churches, and Rees' action was not appreciated by many of his former mission friends who thought he was definitely backsliding. He very quickly made his mark in the Chapel and the elders, recognising the call of God upon him wanted him to enter the ministry. Feeling this was God's will Rees attended the theological college at Carmarthen. He was relieved in many ways that he now felt that God had released him to return to a more normal and natural way of life. When he preached he said very little about the hidden years of his intercession but concentrated on preaching the gospel and stressing new birth, knowing only too well that many in the crowded chapels were still without any assurance of salvation.

In due time their happy marriage was blessed with a son, Samuel. Soon after his birth the bombshell dropped—God was calling them to Africa and it would mean them leaving their precious baby behind. What a price to pay for obedience, especially for Elizabeth! They both wept because they loved him so dearly, but they surrendered baby Samuel into the safe and loving keeping of another uncle of Rees' and turned their faces resolutely towards Africa. Rees spent nine months at Livingstone College in London on a medical course, whilst Elizabeth underwent a year's special training with the Faith Mission in Scotland. They sailed for Africa on July 10th, 1915, to work with the famous South Africa General Mission which had a network of mission stations in many parts of the continent. Rees and Elizabeth were placed at the Rusitu mission station in Gazaland, close to the border with Portuguese East Africa. On their arrival everyone wanted to hear more about the great Welsh Revival of 1904/6. Rees told them that the Holy Ghost was the secret of revival and preached for weeks encouraging them to believe for revival in Rusitu.

As they continued to pray for revival Rees was convinced that their prayer was heard. On Sunday, October 10th (his birthday) the blessing broke. What transpired Rees said was greater than anything he had seen in the Welsh Revival. The whole congregation was in tears; people began to confess their sins and get right with God. Prayer became the order of the day. All who came near the place seemed to come under influence of the Holy Spirit. They had two revival meetings every day for the next fifteen months. When they had made the sacrifice of leaving their baby Samuel, Rees felt that from Christ's promise of a hundredfold compensation he could claim ten thousand souls in Africa. During their six years in Africa he saw that promise fulfilled. After preaching at the Durban Conference of the S.A. General Mission, the directors asked them to visit every one of their forty-three mission stations. At every one of them Rees had a promise from God that He would send revival and He did. They were glorious years of fantastic fruitfulness. Rees and Elizabeth finally came home to Wales on furlough at Christmas, 1920.

The S.A. General Mission were so delighted with the Howells' first term in Africa that they wanted to send them around the world promoting the work of the Mission. It was something which warmed their hearts but as Rees was preaching at the 1922 Llandrindod Wells Convention, God laid on his heart the crying need for a Bible College for the training of young people for the ministry and the mission field. Rees visited the Moody Bible Institute in Chicago during a trip to America shortly after the Convention, and was very impressed. When they were back in Wales, Rees and Elizabeth climbed the much loved slopes of the Black Mountain and knelt to dedicate themselves to the task of building a Bible college. They had just sixteen shillings (80p) between them.

Early in the summer of 1923 while they were enjoying a much needed break in Mumbles, in the vicinity of Swansea, South Wales, God led Elizabeth and Rees to a mansion along the Mumbles Road, which overlooks Swansea Bay. The place was named Glynderwen and as they stood looking over the gate at this manificent property, that inner voice spoke again, 'This is the college!' The purchase of Glynderwen and the establishing of the Bible College of Wales was an exploit of faith from beginning to end. Rees successfully prayed for every pound needed. God revealed to him that he was to pay only £6,150 for it despite the fact that other interested parties were willing to pay £10,000. Against all the odds and after not a few hair-raising moments when all seemed lost, the transaction was completed, the money prayed in, and the college was opened with great rejoicing on Whit-Monday, 1924. A thousand people gathered to witness this tangible miracle of a God who answers prayer and can even provide a mansion set in eight acres of ground!

The first year was an unqualified success; the college gained five tutors and thirty-eight students, but then trouble hit as some began to want to take over and make the college a denominational one. Many walked out and Rees was left with two tutors and five students. So for twelve months there were no lectures while they all devoted themselves to prayer. As a result they started receiving large gifts of money and soon the numbers were back up to six tutors and thirty students. Tuition was provided free and the charge for board and meals was kept to the absolute minimum to encourage all who felt the call of God on their lives to train for His service.

Feeling the burden to expand the college, Rees next launched out with the purchase of a neighbouring property called Derwen Fawr. He walked round it in faith claiming it for the Lord. Eventually, he secured it for £8,000 and it was dedicated at the sixth anniversary of the original college on Whit-Monday, 1930. Over the following years Rees built a College Chapel, a Conference Hall, and student hostels in the grounds. Every penny had to be prayed in. In 1932 God challenged him to establish a school for the children of missionaries: Rees knew only too well the price missionaries paid in having to leave their children behind. He obtained another adjoining property called Sketty Isaf and this was opened as the school for missionaries' children in 1933. Rees had begun the college with only eighteen shillings but in fourteen years he had prayed for and received £125,000! From beginning to end it was an amazing epic of faith with money usually coming in only at the last minute.

On 26th December, 1934 Rees was given a new burden for world missions and the need to get the gospel out to 'every creature' in accordance with the great commission of Jesus in Matthew 28. This heralded the beginning of a new era of spiritual warfare. He shared the burden of this 'every creature' missionary vision with staff and friends of the college, and on New Year's Day 1935 called a day of prayer and fasting. They were to intercede for any nation or country, as well as any missionaries, as the Lord indicated.

With the rise of Hitler and Mussolini, Rees realised that war would be a disaster and a serious setback to world evangelisation, closing many doors. Hitler's occupation of the Rhineland in 1936 was seen as a dangerous threat and for three weeks they prayed and fasted, usually abstaining from food until evening. There was a consciousness of intense satanic opposition and when, after these weeks, there had still been no release in the spirit, Rees received a word from the Lord: 'Prayer has failed and only intercession will prevail.' He called for intercessors who would 'stand in the gap' (Ezek. 23:30), presenting their bodies as living sacrifices to God (Rom. 12:1) to be completely at His disposal and with no more claim on their lives, time or possessions than they would have if they were conscripted into the forces.

Having counted the cost and realised what they were doing, one by one many of the staff and students solemnly laid their lives 'on the altar' as God's intercessors on 29th March, 1936. On the following day, as evidence that their sacrifice had been accepted and the victory gained, the fire of God fell upon them all. For over an hour on their knees all they could do was to sing the chorus, 'Welcome, welcome, welcome! Holy Ghost, we welcome Thee.' From that time on they were welded into a body of committed intercessors.

Mussolini's invasion of Ethiopia was a threat to the evangelisation of that land which the Emperor had been opening up to the gospel. Every yard of the Italian's advance was contested by prayer and intercession, and right to the end Rees believed and declared that they would never enter Addis Ababa. When it fell it was a severe test of faith, but he understood that in such an apparent failure the prayer had gone into 'death' that 'no flesh should glory' and God would bring about a 'resurrection' victory in his own way and time.

So it was not by chance that the exiled Emperor Haile Selassie subsequently visited the Bible College in person and was encouraged when Mr Howells assured him, in the name of the Lord, that he would without fail be restored to his throne. But the greatest outcome of that intercession was seen when in later years S.I.M. missionaries returned to Wallamo Province where they had anxiously left only forty-eight young Christians, and were amazed to find a flourishing church of ten thousand new believers.

God's dealings with Rees Howells and this group of intercessors climaxed in a never-to-be-forgotten Pentecost experience in the New Year of 1937. During those days of Divine visitation the Holy Ghost became a real person to them as never before and they knew that only *He* could fulfil the vision of evangelising the world. They were broken in His presence. The cross was revealed in a new light. A holy hush descended on the place. For three weeks they seemed to lose all sense of time, often praying and worshipping into the early hours of the morning with no thought of bed. From that time many entered into a deeper understanding of spiritual warfare and the purity of heart needed for the Holy Spirit to be able to fight His battles through them.

The burden of the Jews who were suffering increasing persecution under the Nazis came upon Rees at that time. As he searched the Old Testament he saw that prophecies must be believed into manifestation as well as simply uttered (e.g. Dan. 9:2–3). So he began to pray that, in the light of Bible prophecy, the Jews would return to Palestine. Knowing that intercession demanded more than words, his burden for refugee Jewish children caused him to set about establishing a home of refuge for them. The outbreak of war prevented more than a dozen such children being received, but the burden for God's people remained.

In November, 1947 this prayer was to come powerfully upon Rees again when the proposal to partition Palestine and allocate a portion of it to the Jews came before the United Nations Assembly. When votes were first cast the motion failed to gain the required two-thirds majority and the matter was postponed until the following day. Realising that they had not yet 'prayed the matter through', Rees called for an extra time of special prayer that night. In that meeting faith was given and it ended with great rejoicing and assurance of victory. On the following day several countries, including Russia, changed their stance and the second vote showed an ample majority in favour of partition, and a future state of Israel was assured.

Throughout the desperate crises of 1938 when war seemed inevitable, Rees and his little army of intercessors prayed for God to intervene. They were very much aware of the powers of darkness as they engaged in this spiritual warfare; Hitler was known to believe in the occult and the battle was fierce. They rejoiced when Neville Chamberlain returned from Munich with the settlement that promised peace in our time; but things looked very black in 1939. The year's breathing space had given Britain time to prepare somewhat but the situation was serious. Right to the end, Rees Howells believed and publicly declared that there would not be a war. It was an unexpected blow to them all when war *was* declared in September 1939. His detractors were only too ready to mock him and the newspapers joined in the ridicule of 'the false prophet'. Rees, however, accepted it as another 'death' that would lead to a greater resurrection.

Throughout the dark war years of 1939 to 1945, from crisis to crisis, from Dunkirk in 1940 to D-Day in 1944, this select company gave themselves to secret intercession. They were totally committed and were at God's disposal night and day. They responded without question to every call to intercede. Only eternity will reveal their part in the conflict for freedom. The miracle of Dunkirk was accepted by millions as answer to prayer. Throughout those war years this separated company took no holidays but gave themselves to prayer, with often a hundred of them on their knees together. Every day from 7.00 pm to midnight they engaged in prayer—and that after a full day's work, with an hour every morning for prayer, as well as times at mid-day. Frequently they fasted, and many many times they continued long after midnight. They were sustained only by the power of God in a supernatural way as they kept up this level of intercession for years. In many ways Rees Howells was broken by these years of agonising intercession, which at times was so great upon him that he had to remain alone with God. His divinely revealed 'intelligence' of the progress of the war was uncanny; as they prayed about each situation he knew what the outcome would be long before it was announced over the radio.

The end of the war was a great cause for celebration, with the return of the Jews to the new nation of Israel in 1948 a special joy to Howells' heart. His burden remained for the 'every creature' vision and he prayed for a world-wide outpouring of God's Spirit which would make this possible.

As he grew older Rees adopted the belief that he would never actually die, but be 'translated' or swept up to meet Jesus in the air. Although this proved not to be the case and gave his enemies further fuel for criticism Rees Howells' work has lived on and proof of the value of his ministry is embodied in the Bible College of Wales.

Howells eventually suffered a heart attack but refused to slack off in any way. Then on Wednesday, February 8th 1950 in the evening meeting he was filled with joy and quite radiant as they sang 'Away over Jordan with my Blessed Jesus'. He waved his handkerchief as they sang. Half an hour later he suffered another heart attack. As he lay there in agony he gasped 'It is the Lord. I am in the centre of the Lord's will . . . everything is gained.' Four days later on Sunday, February 12th he whispered, 'Victory! Hallelujah!' The end came on Monday, February 13th in Rees' 71st year. His son, Samuel, took over as director of the college and school.

The work continues as an abiding proof to the world that Jehovah-Jireh still provides for all those who, like Abraham, are willing to lay their Isaac (or in Rees' case their Samuel!) on the altar for God. For such intercessors there is always a resurrection waiting just round the corner.

Bibliography

Preface

R. A. Torrey, *The Power of Prayer and the Prayer of Power* Zondervan 1964

George Müller

A. T. Pierson, *George Müller of Bristol* Pickering & Inglis (1972)

A. Rendle Short, *The Diary of George Müller, Selected Extracts* Pickering and Inglis (1954)

F. G. Warne, *George Müller, The Man of Faith* Elim Publishing Co.

J. H. Smith, *Our Faithful God: Answers to Prayer* Marshall Bros. (1911)

E. H. Broadbent, *The Pilgrim Church* Pickering & Inglis (1931)

J. E. Orr, *The Light of the Nations* Paternoster Press (1965)

J. E. Orr, *The Second Evangelical Awakening in Britain* (1949)

R. Steer, *George Müller: Delighted in God* Hodder & Stoughton and STL Books, Bromley (1975)

R. Steer, *A Living Reality* Hodder & Stoughton and STL (1985)

N. Garton, *George Müller and His Orphans* Hodder & Stoughton (1963)

B. Miller, *George Müller Man of Faith and Miracles* Dimension Books, USA (1941)

J. Tallach, *God Made Them Great* Banner of Truth (1974)
The Same Today ... Magazine published by Müller Homes, Bristol

J. Hudson Taylor

M. Broomhall, *Hudson Taylor The Man Who Believed God* China Inland Mission (1929)

I. Burns, *Memoir of the Rev W. C. Burns* Jas. Nisbet & Co. (1875)

M. Broomhall, *Hudson Taylor's Legacy* China Inland Mission (1931)

H. & G. Taylor, *Biography of James Hudson Taylor* OMF Books, London (1965)

M. Broomhall, *By Love Compelled* China Inland Mission (1936)

J. C. Pollock, *Hudson Taylor and Maria* Kingsway (1962)

A. J. Broomhall, *Hudson Taylor and China's Open Century Book Five: Refiner's Fire* Hodder & Stoughton and OMF (1985)

J. E. Orr, *Evangelical Awakenings in Southern Asia* Bethany Fellowship (1975)

K. S. Latourette, *Christianity in a Revolutionary Age Vol 3* Paternoster Press (1970)

Charles Finney

C. G. Finney, *Charles G. Finney an Autiobiography* Salvationist Publishing

C. G. Finney, *Lectures on Revivals of Religion* Fleming H. Revell (1868)

L. A. Drummond, *Charles Grandison Finney and the Birth of Modern Evangelism* Hodder & Stoughton (1983)

L. G. Parkhurst Jr, *Principles of Prayer* Bethany House, USA (1980)

B. Miller, *Charles Finney* Bethany Fellowship Inc. USA (1942)

C. G. Finney, *Power from on High* Victory Press (1943)

C. Clarke, *Pioneers of Revival* Fountain Trust (1971)

J. E. Orr, *The Second Evangelical Awakening in Britain* Marshall, Morgan and Scott (1949)

David Brainerd

J. Page, *David Brainerd Apostle to the North American Indians* John Ritche Ltd. (1936)

J. Edwards, *The Life of Rev David Brainerd (Chiefly Extracted from his Diary)* Baker Book House, USA (1978)

O. S. Smith, *Men of God* Marshall, Morgan & Scott (1971)

W. Searles, *David Brainerd's Personal Testimony (Selected from his Journal & Diary)* Baker Book House, USA (1978)

F. W. Boreham, *A Casket of Cameos* The Abingdon Press (1924)

J. Tallach, *God Made Them Great* Banner of Truth (1974)

Madame Guyon

J Guyon, *Madame Guyon—An Autobiograph* Moody Press

T. C. Upham, *The Story of Madame Guyon's Life* Christian Books, Augusta, USA (1984)

D. G. Coslet, *Madame Jeanne Guyon Child of Another World* CLC, Fort Washington (1984)

J. Guyon, *Union With God* Christian Books, Augusta, USA (1981)

J. Guyon *The Song of Songs* Christian Books, Augusta, USA (1984)

Praying Hyde

Captain E. G. Carré, *Praying Hyde a Challenge to Prayer* Bridge Publishing Inc, USA

F. A. McGaw, *Praying Hyde* Moody Press

J. E. Orr, *Evangelical Awakenings in Southern Asia* Bethany Fellowship (1975)

Rees Howells

N. Grubb, *Rees Howells Intercessor* Lutterworth Press (1973)

D. M. Ruscoe, *The Intercession of Rees Howells* Lutterworth Press and CLC (1983)

J. E. Orr, *Evangelical Awakenings in Africa* Bethany Fellowship (1975)

J. E. Orr, *The Flaming Tongue* Moody Press (1973)